Devon Church Walks
(South and West)

30 Walks

Published by *PP (Pé Publishing)*
Email: tonyhlape12@gmail.com

ISBN: 978-0-9543690-9-5

Maps: John Avenell. Reproduced by permission of Ordnance Survey on behalf of the Controller of Her Majesty`s Stationery Office, © Crown Copyright
Cover Illustration: Audrey Stevens
Photographs: Diana Pé, David Perks and Bonita Tully
Artwork Production: Den Clarke
Printed by: Downland Print Services Ltd, 2015

Acknowledgements: My thanks for their help in the preparation of this book go to John Avenell, Christiane Good, Windy Leung, Anne Parker, Gabrielle and Robert Pe and Giselle, Tony Pe, David Perks, Pam Smith, Audrey Stevens, Peggy Synge, Nicky Thornhill, and Bonita Tully.

I dedicate this book to my friend, Doreen Peskett who shared her knowledge of Nature with me and her love of village churches.

Preface

Regular visitors to Devon come to the county with a mixture of affection and awe. Devonshire has so much natural beauty, so many daunting hills and secluded vales, rich plateaux, wide seascapes and little bays. There are two contrasting coasts: wild and remote in the north; long and varied in the south.

Variety is one of Devon`s main attributes. The very soil is varied; old stones have produced rich culm, then there are four other sandstones, chalk, limestone, red clay and granite. Exeter is at the centre of the contrasting scenery that these stones create. It is also the religious and political capital.

Plymouth is the coastal capital of a seafaring people. Apart from these two, there are few big towns. Axminster in the east and Tavistock in the west are so far apart they emphasize the large extent of the county. In the centre, Crediton has been overtaken by Exeter, and Cullompton by Tiverton. Barnstaple has maintained its dominance in the north – just, for Bideford is a close rival. In the south Totnes has become a cultural centre. We cannot ignore the sprawling Torbay conurbation for retirement and holidays on the south coast and some good walks start there.

Towns and villages are generally far apart. The intervening space is mainly devoted to agriculture. Travellers remember the long, narrow winding lanes, buried deep in hedgerows, bringing them to an exquisite village or lone farm – it may not be the place they were looking for but it is so lovely, the hazards of the travel are worthwhile. Once you have found the starting point for some of the walks in these two books, I hope they help you to unravel some of the ways to church.

Central to each town and village is the parish church often built of local stone. A distinguishing feature of Devon churches can be seen in wooden carvings on many screens and unique bench ends. You will also find long wagon roofs, ancient fonts, beautiful windows and welcoming porches. So many medieval churches, cherished by succeeding generations of Devon men and women, open their doors to the respectful visitor.

I am only sorry I have not included more. There is material here for two more books at least but someone else will have to find the paths, tracks and lanes that I have not taken to the churches I have yet to visit.

Maps: Once again John Avenell has valiently carried on producing carefully clear maps, a double whammy this time, for there are two Devon books!
Covers: Audrey Stevens has chosen a scene from Ilfracombe for the North Devon book and an iconic view of Dartmouth for South Devon. Thank you!

Devon Church Walks

South and West

Location Map

Contents

Introduction

Introduction

Lone farms, interspersed with villages, form the pattern of much of the countryside in Devon. Ever since the Celts started to clear some of the moorland, farming has been a way of life. By the 11th century the shape of the landscape, as it is today, was established. The farmer would have rejoiced in his day of rest on a Sunday, as a break from the unrelenting demands of agriculture. For centuries before and after the Norman Conquest, he would have stood through the Latin Mass in his village church, lulled by the wondrous words. They were familiar to him. If we manage to find an unrestored village church at the end of a long lonely lane, we gain some idea of the blessed sense of sanctuary this building held for the farmer.

The Prayer Book Rebellion. So accustomed was the Devon farmer to the Catholic religious routine, that he did not welcome change. We can only guess what he felt about the Reformation when Henry V111 assumed the authority of the Pope and then ordered the destruction of the monasteries. We do know that he resented any change in the shape of his church service. When the new Prayer Book in English was introduced in 1549, the spark of Rebellion, starting in Sampford Courtenay village (Walk 17), shook the countryside. Farmers advanced on Crediton and, joined by fellow rebels from Cornwall, laid siege to Exeter. Battles were fought and lost. From an estimated 10,000 rebels, 5000 were killed in battle or revenge. Bishop Cranmer described them as 'ignorent men'.

Church Building From Norman Times

There are few plain Norman churches in Devon. Their Norman origins have been obscured by the additional building of the late 13th and early 14th centuries. Even greater transformation came in 15th and 16th centuries when successful merchants spent their wealth on enlarging and reconstructing their church. Norman churches were mainly cruciform with a tower over the crossing. Crediton retains this plan. At Paignton the tower was removed and a replacement built at the west end in 15th century. Some poorer parishes escaped change. Honeychurch is 12th century apart from the tower. Marystow and Brentor are Norman churches. In Cookbury, Bradford, Thornbury and Milton Damerel not much changed in the buildings after 1330. Bradford and Thornbury have 12th century doorways. There are 40 Norman doorways in Devon.

The medieval church in Devon has developed a distinctive character of its own. North and south aisles have often been added to flank the whole length of the church. They absorb the transepts and form chapels on either side of the chancel. The chancel arch may be slight and three parallel wagon roofs have an uninterrupted span of the whole length of the church. These beautiful curved roofs are dotted with seals in the form of carved bosses at intersections. Most churches are Perpendicular with generous windows and five or six bays with piers and arches to match.

Rood Lofts and Screens

The 'Rood' or 'Rode' is the Saxon word for 'Cross'. Early in the Christian Church, a large figure of Christ Crucified on the Cross was often placed near the chancel arch, facing the congregation in the nave. Then a rood loft was introduced to carry candles to light up the Rood. Some of these lofts were quite thick, 6 feet deep even and they had a staircase built up to them. The next development was a screen to separate the chancel from the nave. This was the Rood Sceen. In some churches it ousted the chancel arch. For about 300 years, from the early 14th century, rood screens made a costly demand on the parish. They were also bought for Cathedrals and monastic churches. They serve both to divide the chancel from the nave and to reveal it as a holy place. The screens were carved mainly in wood with some in stone. A few early screens were square framed as at Welcombe. The later screens were arched as at Bradninch. Skilled craftsmen created beautiful works of art with carving, some filigree work and ribbed coving above the arches. There was a wealth of styles. Images of saints were often painted on the lower panels. In Devon Atherington is the only church with a complete Rood loft and screen. At the Restoration most of the roods and lofts were destroyed. Fortunately the screens survived, at least in part. They may have been neglected in 18th and 19th centuries but they have been skillfully restored, where necessary in 20th century.

Religious Houses

(See the introduction in "Devon Church Walks North and East" for more on Saxon and Norman Houses)

Monasteries and Abbeys were scattered throughout Devon, starting with the **Benedictines** in Exeter in 7th century and Tavistock in 974. Buckfast was Cistercian in1018 then Benedictine in1882. The great period for building monasteries arrived in 12th and 13th centuries. Benedictine foundations were at Totnes, Otterton and Pilton. The **Cistercians** built Buckland Abbey in 1278, also Ford Abbey in 1136 – it was then part of Devon. Their houses included Newenham (1245), Dunkeswell (1201) and Exeter. Bishop Warlewast gave Plympton Priory to the Augustinians (1121). The preaching order became powerful and its canons controlled 26 local parishes, appointing vicars and levying fees. It was one of the wealthiest.

Hartland (1169) housed Augustinian canons. Frithelstock Priory, also Augustinian, was founded by Robert Beauchamp in 1229. A **Cluniac** Priory was founded by Judhael in the early 12th century in Barnstaple. Another small Cluniac priory, linked to Montacute was at Kerswell (1119 – 1129). **Premonstratensian** was the order at Torre Abbey, founded by William de Brewer in 1196.

Nunneries were almost exclusively centres of prayer. One was at Polsloe near Exeter: St Katherine`s Benedictine Priory (1160). Two Augustinian nunneries were Canonsleigh (1284) in the north and Cornworthy (13th century) in the south. There were **Friaries**, two in Exeter and two in Plymouth. Friars were inspired by St Francis of Assisi in 1200s. Friars did not acquire wealth and land but went out to preach to the people and lived on donations.

In 12th and 13th centuries Exeter Abbey was converted into a magnificent Cathedral, retaining its original Norman towers. The Bishops of Exeter were powerful men who encouraged the building of parish churches in stone.

Colleges of Clergy were formed. Under Bishop Warelwast (1107 – 1113) 18 secular students, later reduced to 12, attended Crediton College.

In 1327 Bishop John de Grandisson chose Ottery St Mary for the foundation of a collegiate church. It had 40 members; priests, canons and clerks.

Chulmleigh was another collegiate church, formed in 13th century, with 7 prebends. Not all prebendaries were ordained priests. They were employed to pray for the souls of their founders or other luminaries.

In Bere Ferrers, near Plymouth the church was rebuilt to establish a collegiate church, 1330-33. Sir William de Ferrers appointed an archpriest and four other priests, also a deacon.

Slapton College was founded in 1373 by Guy de Brien to train priests for a chantry where they celebrated masses for his soul.

Parishes

Bishops supervised the formation of parish boundaries, so organised that the mother church of the parish had dependent chapels. In later centuries some of these chapels gained the status of parish church.

Parishes were large and houses scattered. The long walk or drive to church along muddy tracks was not appealing in winter. Landowners, who could afford them, applied for licences to build private chapels or oratories. These might be built on their land or as an integral part of their homes.

There were many independent chapelries in Devon. In 1535 Tiverton had 6 chapels. Some chapels later became barns and some disintegrated. Others have grown to be churches. We are privileged to visit such gems as Haccombe, Cockington, Maristow and West Ogwell.

Parishes have continued through good times, when wool and tin brought wealth to the county and through bad times. By the early 19th century, many village churches were dilapidated. Under the strict rule of Bishop Phillpotts, most were severely restored. Those that had a later restoration, such as Hittisleigh and Honeychurch, have retained more of their local character.

Following the enthusiastic builders of the 19th century, when the Victorians put their energies into re-building and also the creation of massive, ornate churches, the emphasis has changed.

Today's keepers of churches honour their history, the authentic expression of past craftsmen and believers. We do not build many churches but local people maintain their church and sometimes have added fine modern glass, wood carving, stone work and painting.

See Introduction to Devon Church Walks North and East for more on the Saxons.

4 Walks near Totnes

Walk 1: Totnes to Berry Pomeroy

From a busy church at the centre of this much loved historic town, we find quiet ways to see the famous castle and the less heeded village church

Starting Point: Totnes Mainline Station   GR802609
Or one of the pay Car Parks on west side of Totnes GR801604
Map: OS Explorer OL20 **Terrain:** Tracks and paths, moderately hilly
Distance: 9 Miles or 6 Miles if you return by bus
Local Information: 1. **Totnes** situated at the highest navigable point of the River Dart, has thrived from 10th century when the town had its own mint. The 16th and 17th centuries were especially fruitful with the export of cloth to France. Merchant houses have survived from this heyday. 2. Totnes has a motte and bailey **Castle** established by the Norman, Judhael. It is open daily in the summer, weekends only Nov.– Mar., closed Christmas and New Year.
3. Home of the Pomeroy then the Seymour families, **Berry Pomeroy Castle** has similar opening times as Totnes. Both are held by English Heritage.
Totnes Castle phone 01803 864406   Berry Pomeroy Castle 01803 866618
Local buses, phone Traveline 0871 200 2233

The Churches
The Parish and Priory Church of St Mary, Totnes is a 15th century building in its entirety. Little remains of an earlier Norman church. There was then a small Benedictine Priory, within the bounds of today`s North Street and South Street. William the Conqueror`s follower, Judhael built it in 11th century. In 1416 work began on a new church but progress was slow and in 1445 monks and townsfolk agreed to hasten the building. The new chancel reached as far as the nave of the Priory and a doorway linked them. (It was blocked in 1869 but the blank east wall was given a window in 1874, designed with 7 lights by Sir Gilbert Scott). To return to 15th century, Bishop Lacy of Exeter provided an incentive in 1434 and nave and chancel were finished soon afterwards. The south chapel of St George has a squint into the chancel to enable people to see the altar. The porch has two storeys and a vaulted ceiling. An ancient

Totnes

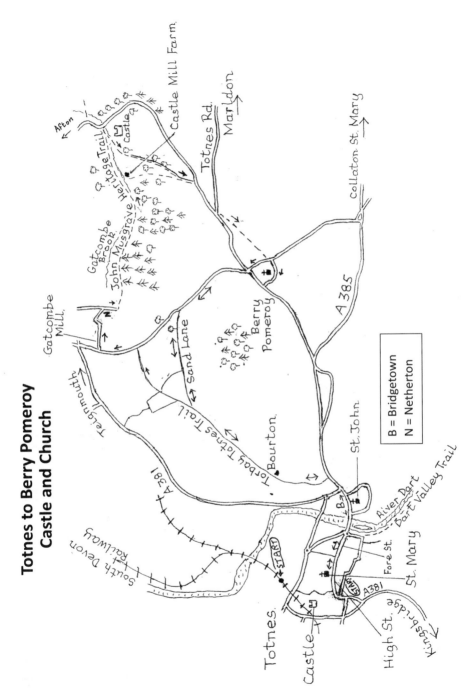

**Totnes to Berry Pomeroy
Castle and Church**

B = Bridgetown
N = Netherton

inner door bears the arms of Bishop Lacy. (In 1620 Christopher Blackhall donated a library to the upper storey. At his death in 1633 a monument was placed on the north side of the nave where he kneels with his four wives below him!) The two great 15th century treasures of this church are: the wide west tower built in red sandstone, work of master mason Roger Growden who based the design on that of Ashburton. It has big octagonal pinnacles and a central turret. Three figures are on the south side. Enter the church for the second treasure: the Beer stone rood screen stretching across the width of the building. It is exceptional with traceried windows and niches that once held figures of saints.

The Church of Berry Pomeroy, St Mary is another 15th century church built on an early site. Sir Richard de Pomeroy (died1496) is believed to have commissioned this building. His may be the tomb on the south side of the chancel. The Seymours are remembered in a monument to Edward, Lord Protector (died 1593). Again the porch has two storeys. The tall tower is plain and rendered so that it is paler than the rest of

Berry Pomeroy

the church. North and south aisles and porch are embattled. The windows are Perpendicular. Inside, the nave is wide. The arcades have leaf frieze capitals. Some have the names of Benefactors. The rood screen has retained some or its original coving and colour. It stretches from north to south walls. Pevsner describes it as one of the most perfect in Devon. The church had two parsons in 100 years: John Prince 1681 – 1723 and Joseph Fox 1723 – 1781.

The Walk

The tower of the Parish Church dominates Totnes, offering you guidance.

With your back to the church entrance, turn left and walk downhill on the High Street. Pass under East Gate Arch and continue down Fore Street.

At crossroads just before the river at the bottom, you will find the bus bay on your left and beyond that the Tourist Information Centre in Town Mill.

Keep on course to cross the River Dart on Totnes Bridge. Keep to the right hand side of the road (there are pavements on both sides). You pass St John`s Church on the right, then a main road on the left. Continue uphill. Shortly after a private road on the left, turn left into Bourton Lane. Signs on the left show John Musgrave Heritage Trail and Torbay Totnes Trail

You are heading north through a residential area. In ¼ mile Bourton Lane leaves the houses behind and descends through fields. At cottages of Bourton Farm, the lane veers right then takes a straight course northwest.

Cross a stream and start climbing. Hedgerows give shelter with occasional gaps offering hillside views. The ground is stony and uneven but generally dry. In 1 kilometre you reach another stony track on the right, Sand Lane. *Note this track as you may return on it. Or you may wish to shorten the walk and turn right here. When you come to the road turn right again. At the main Totnes Road go straight on. The Church is on the right.*

For the full walk, continue climbing on the Trail. Avoid all turnings. Pass some caravans on the side then Combe Park Horse Centre. You reach a road at a T-junction. Turn left and walk along the road for ¼ mile, crossing Gatcombe Brook on the way. Turn right at Gatcombe Mill and walk along a narrow road for another ¼ mile.

At T-junction turn right. You are in Netherton, a few grey houses. At Trail signs turn left away from roads. Gatcombe Brook is down on the left. Wild woodland and small fields abound. Avoid the track marked 'Private'.

Veer right uphill across the field to more Trail signs and enter woodland. Here is a flat path at last! It may be wet in places but still passable. In ½ mile you come to Castle Mill Farm, a neglected inhabited home. Signs point to Berry Pomeroy Castle. Pass the farm on your right to join a tarmac road.

The path shown on the map to the right of the farm was sodden.

From the luxury of the tarmac, you have a delightful view across the stream on the right up through trees to the ruins of Berry Pomeroy Castle. In over ¼ mile, you reach a junction. There are route signs and a display map.

Leave the Trail here. Turn sharp right onto a narrow stony path rising steeply uphill above the Trail that you have just traversed. You come out at the entrance to the Castle on a plateau. Pass the ruins and ticket office on the right to join the driveway to the Castle. *The tearooms were closed in Oct.*

Follow the driveway southwestwards, away from the Castle and downhill for nearly ½ mile. You join the Afton Road and keep on course. Enjoy extensive views as far as Dartmoor on the right and rolling fields on the left.

When you reach the main Totnes Road, cross diagonally right to a footpath leading down towards Berry Pomoroy, seen below. A short track at the bottom brings you on the road with the church nearby.

To walk back to Totnes, turn right on this road. Cross the Totnes Road again. Keep straight on and in 1 kilometre you reach Sand Lane. Turn left here to find the familiar Trail again. Turn left and retrace your steps.

To return by bus, take the little lane that passes below Berry Pomeroy Church up on your right. It brings you back to a lower point on Totnes Road where you may catch Bus 149 back to Totnes.

Walk 2: Cornworthy to Dittisham

From the hilltop make the long descent on the clear trail to follow a stream that enters Dittisham Mill Creek then uphill again for the next church.

Starting Point: Green Close near Cornworthy Church   **GR829556**
Map: OS Explorer OL20   **Terrain:** Hilly, wet in winter
Distance: 6½ or 8 Miles   **Note:** It is a challenge to drive along narrow lanes to the Start. You may find it easier to start the walk at Dittisham but check that Cornworthy pub is open: 01803 732204
Wednesdays at 12.00 and Fridays at 12.30 a shuttle bus leaves Totnes Plains for Ashprington, Tuckenhay and Cornworthy

The Churches

**St Peter`s, Cornworthy** is a light, airy, cream and honey building. It is perfect in its freedom from clutter. All periods of its development have contributed to its beauty. Local stone was transported on the River Dart in 14th century to rebuild this church on the site of an earlier one. St Peter`s still has its Norman font and outside you can still see the north door where the Devil departed. 1350 –1375, the nave arcade has piers of granite monoliths, capitals of Beer stone and limestone arches. The carved wooden rood screen is one of the less ornate. It has carvings of pomegranates recalling Catherine of Aragon and suggesting that it was made before 1533. The tower again is based on that of Ashburton. The Lady Chapel altar is made from granite from the local Priory of St Mary, one of the many destroyed by Henry V111.

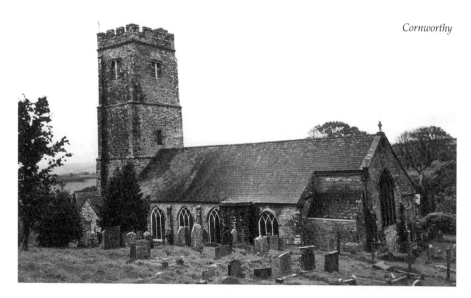

Cornworthy

(Ashprington) Cornworthy to Dittisham

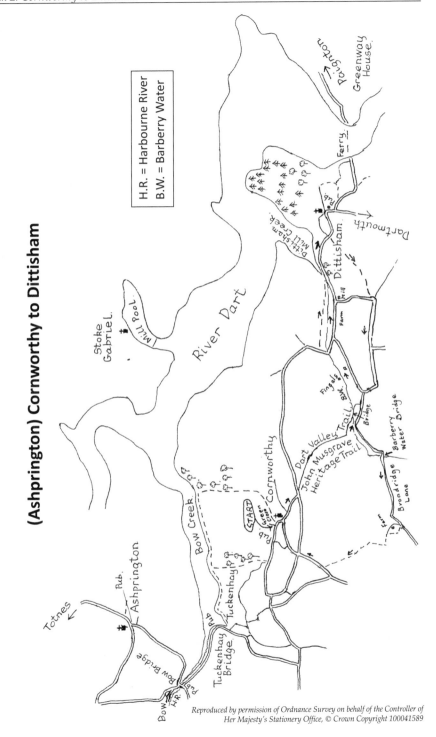

H.R. = Harbourne River
B.W. = Barberry Water

In the chancel there is monument (1611) to Thomas Harris and his wife, who was a Pommeroy, and their kneeling children. The soft brown pews were fitted in 1788. In 1757 John Seale provided the pulpit with a tester, like a canopy. In 1780 the windows were re-framed and fitted with plain glass with coloured edges. The Lady Chapel also has a lovely Angel`s Wing of 1997. The good cream floor, laid last year, fits so well in this church. Charles Barter was vicar here for 71 years, 1775 – 1846.

Cornworthy

St George`s, Dittisham has the mark left by its Norman predecessor on the east face of the tower. The tower, probably the oldest part of the present building would have been a sea defense. The Norman font of red sandstone and key pattern on flutings is similar to that of Rattery. The church itself was built of local ashlar 1328 – 1333. Bishop Grandisson dedicated it to St George. The pinnacled porch has two storeys. The priest could keep an eye on the church from a window in the first floor. Dittisham has been fortunate to retain its 15th century stone pulpit when other churches lost theirs, destroyed by Oliver Cromwell`s men. It has 5 canopied niches and shafts ornamented with leaves and grapes. The rood screen`s canopy was removed in Elizabeth 1`s reign. However, Herbert Read replaced loft and canopy in 1954. The glass in the east window may be by Pugin but this has not yet been confirmed.

Dittisham

The Walk

Facing Cornworthy Church walk to the right and climb along a lane that goes up behind the church. In 100 metres at crossroads go straight over to the Trail, shared by Dart Valley and John Musgrave, Broadgates Lane.

It starts beside bungalows and a chicken farm then descends on a stony, fern-lined track under trees. A stream flows beside the track (on our October venture overflowed onto it). After a while it flows away and we have the descent to ourselves. In 1 kilometre the path, now less steep, turns left and crosses a little bridge over Barberry Water. It turns right and comes to a T-junction at **Barberry Cross.**

Turn left to join the tarmac lane. You are heading northwest and pass a hotel, 'Fingals'. At the next junction you have a choice: *Either turn left and follow the Trail downhill to cross a stream, keep on the road for 100 metres then turn right and walk above the stream, now down on your right.*

Or turn right and walk along the high-banked lane to Brambletorre Mill. The Lane veers left and joins the Trail route at Dittisham Mill Creek.

Both routes continue on the road past Mill Copse and up to Higher Street. Dittisham Church can be seen ahead. The Pub/Post Office/Village Stores/BB is just around the corner to the right – beware of the temptation to relax here!

From Dittisham Church retrace your steps along Higher St. for ¼ Mile. Just after the road on the right, turn left to the footpath in the hedge.

Higher Dittisham, view over River Dart

Go through to high, open fields and up to a field gate. There are views over the River Dart. Follow the hedge on the left for ½ mile walking downhill. When the hedge ends, veer right and more steeply downhill. Pass a little copse on the right and leave the field by a gate on the left.

You have arrived at a road junction. Go straight on uphill heading east along this pleasant lane with hill views. At Kingston Cross pass a road on the left. Follow your lane as it bends to the right and goes past a lone cottage

At the next junction turn left. *You* are back at the familiar **Barberry Cross**

For the shorter route, turn right and retrace your steps uphill on Broadgates Lane following the Trail back to Cornworthy.

For the longer route, go straight on along this farm track, Broadridge Lane. It runs parallel to and follows the curve of Barberry Water on the right. In ½ mile it turns right to cross at Barberry Water Bridge and heads eastwards to Broadridge Farm. You turn right joining the road here for a little way. Then cross to the footpath that heads mainly north uphill with some zigzags at the start. After woodland, veer right towards a field corner. Cross to the next field and follow the hedge on the left. In the last field the hedge on the right leads you to Southills Farm and the tarmac Lane. Turn right for Cornworthy At crossroads go straight over to the Church. *If you wish to view the Priory Ruins turn left and follow Water Lane then curve right along Abbey Road to pass through the main village, with pub and the Church.*

Walk 3: Rattery to Tigley Cross, Brooking Church and Harberton

Walk over hills to find churches just two or three miles apart but standing in different worlds

Starting Point: Rattery Church – Car Park shared with the pub **GR**741616
Map: OS Explorer OL20 **Terrain:** Paths and lanes climb over the hill **Distance:** 8 Miles (3 ½ on lanes) **Note:** If you wish to avoid some lanes, try the walk in two sections and drive from Tigley to Blakemore.
Brooking Church, Tigley Cross has a small car park.
Local Information: 1. Church House Inn, Rattery is so old (11th century) that it housed the first builders of the Church.
2. Church House Inn, Harberton dates from 1100. It was a chantry house for monks and retains some original timbers.

The Churches
The Church of St Mary the Virgin, Rattery stands in an elevated village. Outside it is dark and gloomy with a slim pointed tower. Inside, it is bright and colourful. The guide book gives a summary of its history: 'The font, nave and sanctuary speak of the 12th century; the tower, narrow aisles and probably the transepts were added

about the 13th, the Chancel Chapels are 15th century; the spire, too, could be of this time'. The guide book also explains the unusual internal decoration, known as 'Sgraffito' that bathes the church in colour. Originating in ancient Greece and popular in Italy, it is a technique based on scratching a surface to reveal the lower layer. It came to England in 1870s and the owners of the local Marley estate, the Carews, brought it to this church. Despite changes over the ages, including the enlargement of the chancel in 1460, the 15th century rood screen and the insertion of larger windows in 13th and 15th centuries with later Victorian glass, the church still has the feel of a Norman building. The rare Norman font of red sandstone and a bowl with shallow flutings, is similar to that of St George`s, Dittisham.

Rattery

    Brooking, St Barnabas is a Victorian church in the style of Pugin who promoted the Gothic Revival. The Chapernowne family from Dartington Hall saw to its completion in 1855. It has a long chancel,

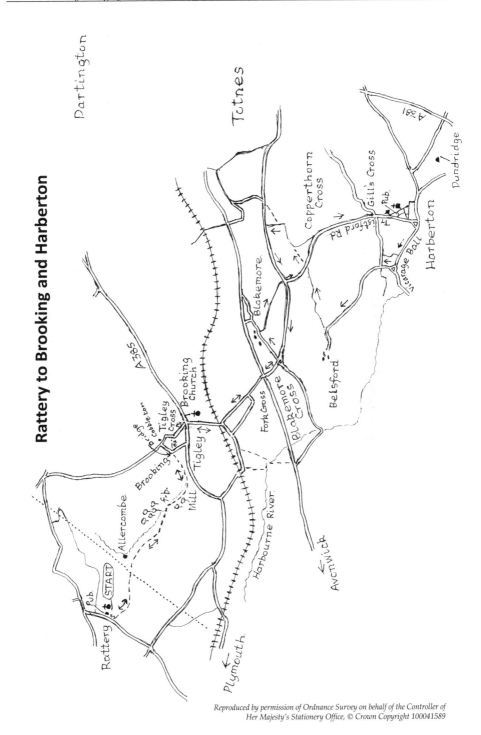

Rattery to Brooking and Harberton

nave with aisle and tower on the south side. The south arcade has two massive grey marble pillars, lit by the tower window. The marble had been exhibited in The Great Exhibition of 1851 and admired by Queen Victoria. Medieval buildings took years to erect; 19th century Gothic could be completed in a few months. The rest of the interior is in Caen stone. Concerts are held here occasionally.

St Andrew`s Church, Harberton stands on a holy site. It is a splendid Perpendicular church, built in 14th – 15th centuries and was an administrative centre, more important than Totnes. This large village in fertile country had a chapel in Saxon times. The church still has its Norman font, carved in red sandstone. The tower is of the favoured Ashburton Style. The porch has two storeys with carvings of heads in the vaulted ceiling – Edward 1 (1272-1307) and Eleanor? Inside, the spacious nave has a fine barrel roof (1370) with eighty carved bosses representing legendary figures. The north and south aisles have six bays. The large windows are

Harberton

filled with colourful Victorian glass, so the church is bright and sumptuous. The 15th century rood screen has exceptionally beautiful vaulting and cornices. The original panels were replaced in 1871 by metal ones. The thirteen original panels can be seen in glass cases, north in the nave. The Medieval stone octagonal pulpit with carved foliage is also 15th century and one of the best in Devon. The little statues were fitted probably in 17th century to replace those that were no doubt damaged in the Reformation. The Harvey family of Dundridge is remembered in this church. Theirs is the largest box pew. One touching memorial depicts the 10 year old boy, Robert Harvey on a bed of marble, 1895. Known as Tito, he was born in Peru, his mother`s homeland.

The Walk
Leave Rattery Car Park and turn left to walk down the lane for 50 metres. Turn left into a public right of way that follows a cinder farm track. Head eastwards towards Allercombe Farm. Soon after walking under power cables, you leave the track that descends to the left to the farm.

You turn right into a rough stony track under trees. In 100 metres come out of the wood and stop! The track veers to the right. Avoid it and go straight on to a double gate. Go through the pedestrian gate on the right. You are at the top of a slope on a natural grassy ledge following the hedge on the right. A stream runs through the valley at the bottom of the slope. You are heading southeast. The sense of the remoteness of this valley is dispelled by the sound of passing trains on the main line.

At woodland, head down to the valley and cross the stream on a footbridge. The stream flows to the right to feed the Mill. The path takes you to the left through the wood. In 150 metres you emerge, turn right and follow the edge of the wood on your right. You come to the access lane to the Mill. Turn left on this lane to Brooking where the former parsonage stands. Cross a stone bridge to cottages. Keep on course to Cobbleton. Turn right towards the main road, A385 at 'Tigley Cross'. **Note the lane** opposite.

Cross with care to the left of the **lane**. The entrance to Brooking Church is off the main road. After visiting the church, walk up the noted **lane**. It goes over the railway line on a road bridge. Keep straight on, southeastwards still, to 'Fork Cross'. *Totnes is to the left*. Again cross to the lane opposite. In 250 metres you come up to the triangle of roads at 'Blakemore Cross'.

Turn left here to the cluster of houses at Blakemore. The lane bends to the right then left. At this bend turn right into a track that climbs steeply up the hillside. When you are nearly over the brow you come to a T-junction. Cross diagonally right to join Tristford Road down to Harberton. This is a pleasant lane offering views over the countryside below. In over 1 mile you come down to the edge of the village of Harberton and fork left for the church.

From Harberton Church go in front of the neighbouring pub and carry on down to the road that passes through this attractive village. Follow this road to the right and start climbing along Vicarage Ball. In 300 metres you reach a triangle of roads and turn right into the no through road to Belsford. *Hedges on either side obscure views but this quiet lane, dry under foot, takes you quickly back up to the hill behind Harberton.*

Avoid turnings and keep heading northwest for a kilometre. Here the road curves left to Belsford. You turn right into a track under trees. You soon emerge from the trees and find you are up in the hills heading northeast.

In 500 metres you reach the familiar Tristford Road *Harberton is down to the right*.

To return to Rattery, cross to the footpath opposite and follow the arrow directing you diagonally left across an elevated field with distant views over countryside ahead. Too soon you reach another enclosed track. Turn left here and the track takes you on a bendy way for 350 metres to a T-junction.

Turn left on this lane and in 1 mile you are back at Blakemore Cross. Turn right here and retrace your steps over the 'Totnes Road', over the railway line and over the main road to Brooking. The signpost indicates 'Cobbleton'. Retrace your steps by re-crossing the stone bridge to the woods and fields and valley stream that leads you back to the cinder track to Rattery.

Walk 4: National Trust Car Park, Little Dartmouth - Castle Point - Dartmouth - Stoke Fleming optional extra

A scenic seaside and harbour walk to a historic port and three fine churches

Starting Point: National Trust Car Park off A379, south of Dartmouth
GR874492 Map: OS Explorer OL20 **Terrain:** Some hills, esp. on coast
Distance: 6 Miles (+ 3 Miles if you walk to Stoke Fleming and back)
Local Information: Dartmouth Castle 1488-94 was built to guard the estuary. In times of war this could be blocked with a heavy chain. The Castle is open daily except Nov. to Mar. when it opens weekends only.
 Phone English Heritage 01803 833588
Dartmouth was first mentioned in 1049 in the Saxon Chronicle. Crusader ships left from here in 12th century. Much early success as a port diminished after the Civil War. Prestige returned with the building of the Royal Naval College 1899. Craft left from here for D-day landings in World War 2. Now the sailing vessels are recreational. No railway came to Dartmouth and it has been spared industry. Instead, summer traffic clogs the approach roads.
Cherub Inn was built in 1380 near the new Town Church.

The Churches

St Petrox, the Castle, Dartmouth was originally a little chapel, one of many along the coast. It shone a light at the mouth of the Harbour. In 1349 it was for the people of 'South Town', and linked to the Parish Church of Stoke Fleming. In 1438 Bishop Lacy offered 40 days` indulgence to those who would build and maintain the Chapel of St Petrox. At that time the Carews held the nearby Manor and some parishioners lived in the Parish of Warfleet. The south aisle may have been the extent of this chapel. The north aisle was added in 1641. The early 17th century was a time of prosperity for Dartmouth. After rebuilding their own church, they set to on St Petrox and built the tower with spire 20 feet high, two arcades and the Gothic windows on the north side. During the Civil War the Church was used as a provision store, but unlike the Manor House, it did survive. In 1856 the spire was removed. The Church houses a beautiful 12th century font, circular with palmette frieze It has come from elsewhere and has found a fitting home.

   **St Saviour`s, Dartmouth** is a busy place in the centre of town. It was not always so. In 13th century the newly settled folk near the shore had to trudge uphill to St Clement`s. They appealed to King Edward 1 who allowed them to build a church nearer home but the Bishop refused permission. In 1335 they built an oratory. Finally in 1372 Bishop Brantyngham recognised the new church and consecrated it. Meanwhile, a tower was added and a magnificent wooden south door. Today the door, dated 1340, is on display. It is embellished with the tree of life and two leopards. There are some exceptional brasses including one in the chancel of John Hawley with a wife on either side. He was a merchant trader who helped protect Dartmouth; he was also a pirate. He died in 1408. In 15th century arcades may have been partly rebuilt in the

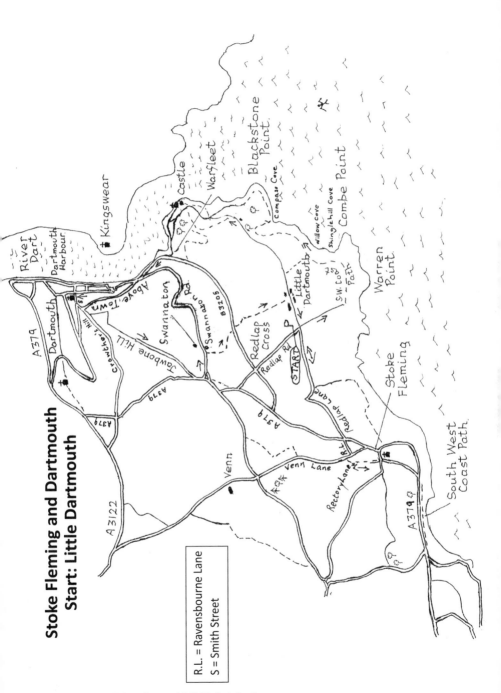

Stoke Fleming and Dartmouth
Start: Little Dartmouth

R.L. = Ravensbourne Lane
S = Smith Street

St Petrox, the Castle, Dartmouth

St Saviours's, Dartmouth

Perpendicular style. Southwest bays are older, perhaps part of the original oratory. The rood screen was fitted in 1480. It is a beautiful piece of oak carving with fan vaulting, perfect coving and paintings of saints in the lower panels. The colourful stone pulpit, added in 1495 makes a remarkable impact today and must have bowled over earlier congregations. In 1620 a porch was fitted to replace the two-storey original. The church was restored 1633–7 and a west gallery installed. There are rose windows at either end of the gallery. Visitors to this Church include Geoffrey Chaucer who probably drew on one of the piratical mariners remembered here, as his model for the 'Shipman'. I

have only skimmed the surface, there is much more of interest in this lovely church.

Stoke Fleming, St Peter standing near the mouth of the River Dart has long been a navigation mark. It has a Norman font from an earlier church. Near this font is a late 13th century effigy of Lady Elyenore Mohun who founded the church. She was a

Stoke Fleming

descendant of Reginald Mohun. The Mohuns had succeeded the Flemings as Lords of the Manor. Richard the Fleming had given his name to 'Stoc', as mentioned in Domesday. Elyenore married into the Carew family. The Carew arms are over the chancel arch. The tall 13th century tower dominates the village and countryside around. As at Totnes, the tower of Ashburton was chosen for a model. The transepts of the first cruciform church were absorbed in the aisles in 14th century. Inside, different types and colours of stones make up the bays and they were heightened in 15th century. The brass to John Corp (died 1361) and his granddaughter (died 1391) is the second oldest in Devon. The excellent wood carvings are more recent. In 1891 Violet Pinwell aged 17, carved animals and Bible scenes on the pulpit. A thorough Victorian restoration of 1871 changed the character of the church. The windows date from 1866.

The Walk
Redlap Road gives access to the Car Park, Little Dartmouth
Two Routes to Dartmouth:
    1. *Shorter, easier route:* *Turn left towards the hamlet of Little Dartmouth and follow the* *track* *northeastwards to Castle Point – just over 1 mile.*
    2. The picturesque coastal route (with escape paths to the **track**): Head south towards the coast. This path is enclosed at first but soon opens to coastal downs. Head

towards Combe Point and turn left so that you are above Shinglehill Cove. In another ¼ mile you climb above Willow Cove *to the first escape path. A stream pours down to the sea here.*

Dartmouth from Castle Point

Avoiding the escape path, turn right and saunter along cliff tops towards Compass Cove. Continue through scrubland to a fork in the ways. I prefer to turn left here rather than plunge down to Nancy`s Chasm.

If you wish to see the old cable house at Compass Cove and carry on to Blackstone Point, you have to take the right fork.
    Avoiding Compass Cove, turn away from the coast to follow the slightly defined path uphill beside a hedgerow on the left then veer right to join the **track** (Little Dartmouth is to the left). Your route is to the right, northeast along the **track** to Coastguard Cottages.

You have fine views over Dartmouth Harbour to Daymark on the far side.
    Follow the tarmac lane from the cottages, gently downhill. Avoid all turnings to left and right until you come to steps down to Dartmouth Castle. Here, below the tearooms and castle stands St Petrox Church.
    From St Petrox follow the tarmac approach road or climb to the Coast Path running

Dartmouth Castle, River Dart

parallel to the road. Continue down to Warfleet Creek. *Some houses here have been built on the beach.* You veer right, joining the B3205.

This is Warfleet Road. The pavement on the left rises above the road and passes a colourful assortment of merchants` houses with sea views.

Avoid the left fork to 'Above Town'. Instead keep straight on. Pass the Catholic Church on the left. Ahead you can see the tower of the Town Church. Fork left into Higher St and pass the Cherub Inn on the right. The Town Church, St Saviour`s is nearby ahead. *The Waterfront is to the right, the Market and more of the old town is behind the Church.*

**To return to Car Park from St Saviour`s** turn uphill away from the Waterfront. From Smith Street start climbing Crowther`s Hill, the old road into Dartmouth.

'Above Town' is the first turning to the left. If you wish to return the way you came, turn left and go back down to Warfleet Road.

For the inland route go up to the next left turn, a no through lane with good views over the Harbour. The lane turns sharp right up Jawbone Hill on a track with some tarmac. Pass a tower on the right and continue to a triangle of roads at A379. Turn left into Swannaton Road then right into a track to Higher Weekes. This leads to Weeke Hill. Turn left at T-junction then immediately right into a track southeast down to Little Dartmouth. Turn right for the Car Park.

To continue to Stoke Fleming, keep straight on heading west along Redlap Lane. In 1 mile you come to A379 again. Cross the main road diagonally left to Ravensbourne Lane. At T-junction with Cinders Lane turn right then left into Rectory Lane where an alley leads to a back road to the Stoke Fleming Church. Retrace your steps to the Car Park.

Walk 5: Slapton to Torcross, Beesands and Stokenham

A varied walk from a Nature Reserve with an inland lake, a shingle bank by the sea, a cliff climb and descent to a small seaside resort and a rural return

Starting Point: Layby, Sands Road, just below the Field Study Centre **GR**824447
Map: OS Explorer OL20   **Terrain:** Varied, some hills
Distance: 11 Miles, can be shortened, using hourly buses
Local Information: 1. Slapton Ley Field Centre covers 460 acres including a fresh water lake, wet meadow and woodland and 2 miles of shingle ridge formed by the sea after the last Ice Age. **Phone** 01548 580685
2. Slapton College was founded in 1373 by Guy de Brien to train priests for a chantry where they celebrated masses for the soul of the founder. They had a chapel of St Mary. In1545 Henry V111 suppressed all chantries. In 1551 Sir Thomas Arundell acquired the house, once a chantry for himself. Today, a tower, all that remains of the chantry, stands in Slapton.
3. Torcross takes its name from a Tor or rock at the end of the beach.
In 13th century 'Stoke in Hamme' distinguished it from other Stokes.

The Churches
Beesands, St Andrew was built in 1883 as a mission room for fishermen. It is a single cell chapel standing white and bright on the beach next to a shack selling meals and foodstuffs – a delightful seaside scene.

Beesands

Slapton to Beesands and Stokenham

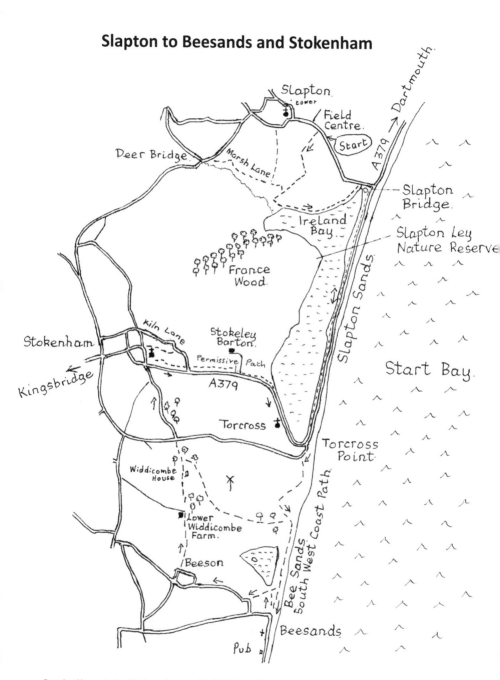

Stokenham, St Michael and All Angels is a grand Perpendicular church on the side of a hill overlooking Start Bay. The church is near a holy well that used to overflow into a pond. The car park now occupies the pond space. The church still has the Norman granite font with marks where a cover was secured to prevent theft of the holy water for witchcraft. The nave, late 15th century, has north and south aisles. The arcades are built of Beer stone that was transported by sea. Each capital has a different design carved on it. The north pier by the tower has a green man. The wagon roof with carved bosses extends the length of the church. The 16th century carved wooden rood screen extends the width of the church. The transepts were originally chapels; each contains a piscina (for washing the communion vessels). The chancel has

Stokenham

undergone much Victorian restoration when a double piscina was discovered walled up. It is quite rare, dating from the reign of Edward 1 (1272 –1307) and has been fitted into the restored wall. The church still has chapels on either side of the chancel. The north chapel contains the organ. The south or Holdsworth chapel has a table believed to have replaced the stone altar during Elizabeth 1`s reign (1558 – 1603). The tower, again Ashburton in style, was rebuilt in 1636. There are large louvres to let out the sound of the bells that may have warned of the approaching Spanish Armada

Slapton, St James the Greater is a medieval church in the centre of an ancient village; 'Sladonia' in Domesday. There has always been a rich agricultural valley here with good red Devonshire soil. A church is mentioned in 1292 and Bishop Stapleton of Exeter dedicated the High Altar in 1318. The stone from this original altar was discarded probably during the Reformation. It has been found. It has a cross on each corner and a Maltese cross in the centre. This ancient stone is now built into the existing altar. The 14th century chancel has two Early English windows. The nave and aisles were built 75 years later with Perpendicular arcades. The two storey porch has two windows above the north door – the priest could see who was coming. There is a sanctuary ring inside the porch. Up until 1623, fugitives could gain sanctuary by touching this stone. They then had to obey exacting church rules. The west tower has a plain broach spire. There are now six bells. At the end of 19th century the church was in a ruinous state. The vicar, Revd. H.G. Warner, supported by parishioners, took 20 years to repair and strengthen it. In 1943 the village and

surrounding area were
evacuated to allow U.S. forces
to practice for the Normandy
landings. After the War, mine
detectors were used before
people were allowed to
return. The south wall of the
church had been hit so that
repair of masonry and
woodwork was needed. The
rood screen had been
removed to safety. It was
replaced 'clumsily' according

Slapton

to Pevsner. No doubt villagers, reclaiming their houses and land after war damage,
neglect and rats, did their best for the church.

The Walk

Walk a little way up Sands Road towards but not as far as the Field Centre. Turn left
to enter the Nature Reserve at a five bar gate. This is public footpath. It starts on
tarmac and is shared with South Grounds Farm. In ¼ mile pass a pond on the left
then turn right through woodland.

Nature Reserve, Slapton

In ½ mile avoid a turning to the right. Follow the path as it soon swings to the left
and takes you beside the lake, Slapton Lee. *Here you may spot Great Crested Grebes,
Tufted Duck and Coots feeding on the many fish.*

After seats and a picnic area you come up to the road at Slapton Bridge.

Cross A379 to the beach where you can catch a bus to Torcross.
Or turn right to walk on the footpath parallel to sea and road for 1½ Miles.

At Torcross turn left beside a block of seaside flats towards the beach then immediately right to find the South West Coast Path. You have a steep climb with many steps and occasional viewpoints.

Keep straight ahead at the cliff top then veer to the right to woodland. Here the path curves and heads downhill steeply. *A woodland path on the right cuts out Beesands.* The last part of the descent has steps down to the coastal plain. The village of Beesands is in view and a lake nearby. Here is a welcome flat promenade and a cheerful little seaside resort. You pass toilets on the way to the food shack, the church and then the pub.

From Beesands to Stokenham walk back to the promenade that brought you here. Cross to the private road running parallel to the promenade. Pass a few detached white houses that look out to sea. At the end of the private road turn left into a footpath that leads steeply uphill on the edge of a field. The hedge is on your left. The coast road from Beesands is also on the left.

Emerge to the coast road and turn right to continue uphill. High hedges now obstruct your view. In under ½ mile the white lines on the edge of the coast road are interrupted. Turn right here into the hamlet of Beeson.

Follow the lane as it makes a loop through this small residential area. At a second bend you turn right into a track for campers. This is also a public right of way. It heads north through woodland then climbs to a junction with the farm track at Lower Widdicombe Farm, about ½ mile from Beeson. Look back to views.

Cross diagonally right to a footpath that leads steeply uphill on the edge of a wood on your right. You are still heading northwards. In ¼ mile you come to the deserted walled garden of Widdicombe House and continue through woodland with the remnants of a tree house. *It is as if the Edwardian owners of this land had vanished and left their home to nature.*

At crosspaths follow the sign to 'Widewell', that is straight on. You come almost immediately to a road junction. Cross to the narrow enclosed lane opposite. It leads downhill passing a nature trail in the woodland on the right and curves down to come out opposite Stokenham Church. You have a good view of this handsome building towards the end of your descent.

To return to Slapton from Stokenham
Either wait for bus at the bus stop seat outside the Church by the A379
Or face the Church and turn right into a footpath that runs parallel to the road and heads eastwards. In ¼ mile you come to trees then Kiln Lane. Cross to the permissive path past the caravan site. In another ¼ mile you pass the access road to Stokely Barton. The permissive path now continues beside the road down to Torcross. Return to Slapton along the beach and back to the layby on Sands Road.

The bus should drop you near the Field Centre on Sands Road.

To visit Slapton Church continue up Sands Road to the village. Pass the village stores on the left. At the nearby road junction turn right to the church.

The old chantry tower looms ahead but the Church is down on the left.

5 Walks near Newton Abbot

Walk 6: Newton Abbot, Country Bus 176 to Denbury
Denbury to West Ogwell (East Ogwell)
and Newton Abbot

This is a linear walk from village churches and along the wooded banks of the River Lemon to the historic St Leonard`s Tower, Newton Abbot

Starting Point: Bus Station, Sherborne Road near the Market Newton Abbot
GR860714   **Map:** OS Explorer 110
Terrain: fields, hills, riverside   **Distance:** 5 ½ Miles
Local Information: Country Bus 176 leaves Newton Abbot (not Sundays) 9.45, 10.45 and 11.45 for Denbury   Phone traveline 0871 200 22 33
St Leonard`s Tower was once part of a chapel of ease to Wolborough where monks from Torre Abbey (1196) had a settlement. The old chapel was on the east side of

St. Leonard's Tower, Newton Abbot

the tower. The tower, 13th century and probably the oldest building in Newton Abbot, is built in two stages in grey limestone. William of Orange declared his intention of claiming the British Throne here in 1688. Today`s visitor can climb the tower for a view of the town.

Bradley Manor, beside the River Lemon, is also 13th century and retains its medieval character. The chapel and hall are early 15th century. The National Trust cares for this manor, open April to September, 10.30 a.m. – 5 p.m. Tuesdays, Wednesdays and Thursdays.   Phone 01803 661907

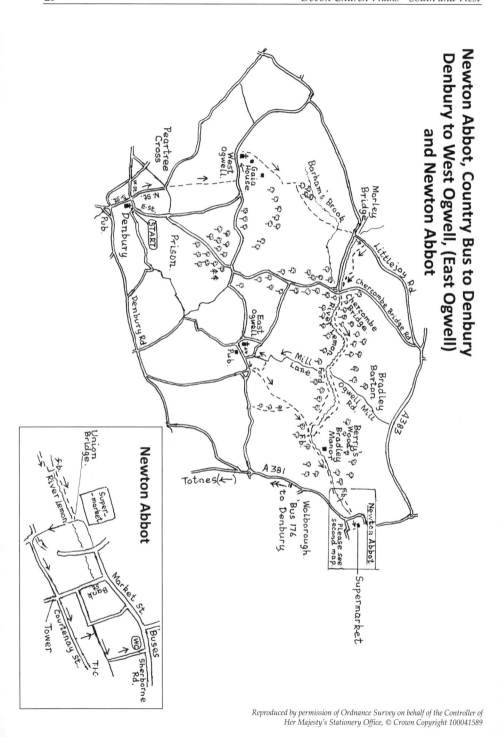

Newton Abbot, Country Bus to Denbury Denbury to West Ogwell, (East Ogwell) and Newton Abbot

The Churches

Denbury, St Mary the Virgin is late 13th century. The church with no aisles is cruciform and still has a musicians` gallery. The long chancel is the oldest part. The east window has intersecting tracery. The glass depicting the baptism, crucifixion and ascension of Christ is by Wailes. The side windows are double lancets. The medieval screen in the north transept came from the old church of Dartington. The screen in the south transept was made in 1988 by a villager. The two stage west tower is 62 feet high. The Norman font is of pink sandstone.

West Ogwell is in the care of the Churches Conservation Trust. One of few early medieval churches, it has not changed. It stands on a remote knoll with only the former manor house of 1790 for company. The cruciform church was built around 1300 and has retained its medieval roof. Tower and transepts have round arches. It has a 13th century sedilia. The windows are late 13th century. The tower was added in 1400. The pulpit is Jacobean. The box pews are Georgian. No Victorian restoration has changed the character of this church.

East Ogwell, St Bartholomew by contrast is at the centre of the village. Built in mid 15th century, this church consists of nave, chancel, north aisle, south transept, tower with polygonal stair turret and south porch where there is a fire place. The tower and south window in the chancel may be Early English. There is an early 15th century rood screen and a 17th century tower screen. The Perpendicular piers of the north aisle are similar to those of Bishopsteignton. The chancel floor was raised and the roofs rebuilt in the Restoration of 1885. Richard Reynell's tomb is in south transept. He was Sheriff of Devon (died 1585). An Early Christian burial stone is inscribed Caoci Fili Poplici, 'Caocus, son of Peblig', a chieftain who died circa 500 A.D. This 6th century stone in two halves is set in the east and west gables.

East Ogwell

The Walk

There are no refreshment opportunities (even the pub at East Ogwell does not always open for lunch) so take your own!

From Denbury Church walk up North Street for ¼ mile to Peartree Cross. Continue northwards for ½ mile on the footpath up to West Ogwell. At tarmac road turn left for the Church.

From West Ogwell Church, after enjoying the view all around, take the footpath northeastwards. This hilly part of the walk in one mile brings you to a track over Barham`s Brook. Half way along the path takes a plunge to the left towards woodland and then to the right to resume its course northeast.

After Barham`s Brook you come to crossroads. Keep straight on along Littlejoy Road, over Morley Bridge then turn right into a footpath down to the River Lemon. This little river is favoured with footpaths leading back to Newton Abbot, a distance of 2 ½ - 3 miles.

From Morley walk beside the little River Lemon for ½ mile to Chercombe Bridge. Stay on the north side of the river and look across to the woodland on the other side. In 1 kilometre you reach Ogwell Mill Road and decision.

To visit East Ogwell Church and village, turn right here and cross the River Lemon at a ford. Follow Mill Lane southwards for ½ mile to the edge of the village. Pass Croft Road on the right and continue down to Ogwell Road where you turn right for church and pub. (Church was open and pub closed when I was here).

From East Ogwell return to Ogwell Road and turn left away from the church. Climb uphill past houses to the elevated village green on the left. Note the finger post and follow the direction on the finger to the right.

Cross to the corner of the green and into the next field where you follow the hedge northeastwards. You come to a space above woodland. Many paths cause confusion. Veer slightly to the right to a V-shaped inlet into the wood. Make for another finger post on your right. You are at a T-junction.

*Turn left and walk down through the wood to another T-junction. Turn left and follow the track as it curves to the right and down to the river. Turn right towards Newton Abbot. You are on the south bank of the river. In ¼ mile you come to a **sturdy footbridge over the river**.*

To omit East Ogwell, ignore the instructions in italics above. You still have a choice: either cross the ford and turn left on the south bank or keep on course on the north bank. In 1 kilometre you reach **a sturdy footbridge over the river.**

Now is your opportunity to visit Bradley Manor on the north side of the River Lemon, provided you have chosen Tuesday, Wednesday or Thursday. (See Notes above).

From Bradley Manor return to the south side, via the sturdy footbridge and turn left to continue to Newton Abbot, now only ½ mile away. On the way you pass paths to the right up to Wolborough (the church here is only open on Sundays when the bus 176 does not run!)

On the outskirts of Newton Abbot you have to cross a footbridge and walk on the north bank. As you enter the town, at a supermarket on the left, turn right over Union Bridge and walk across the store car park to St Leonard`s Tower (See above under 'Local Information').

To return to the Bus Station, walk along Courtenay Street and turn left. Go through the market to Sherborne Road. (TIC is at the end of Courtenay Street).

Walk 7: Broadhempston to Torbryan

The shortest walk may lead to the loveliest church

Starting Point: The Square, Broadhempston   **GR**802663
Map: OS Explorer 110   **Terrain:** Village street to gentle field slopes
Distance: 3 Miles.
A lane walk from Torbryan via Orley Common adds at least ½ Mile
Local Information: 1. Nearby Orley Common has undisturbed ancient woodland and grassland. Paths are south of the Orley Common Car Park.
2. Am Brook is a tributary of the River Dart
3. Old Church House Inn, Torbryan dates from around 1400. It became a busy stage coach inn on route between Exeter and Plymouth. It went into decline with the end of stage coaches. Fortunately in 1938 Howell Paine rescued and restored the inn.
4.The Monk`s Retreat in Broadhempston, now a pub, was probably also a church house. There is an arch over the church entrance with a room above.

The Churches

Broadhempston, St Peter and St Paul, was once dedicated to St Petrock. The village takes its name from a Saxon 'Haema' and a Norman 'Borhard'. From the first stone church, built in 1221 by William de Canteloupe, only the base of the tower and the chancel walls remain. In 1400 the village benefitted from the cloth and tin trades and was able to build a bigger church with north and south aisles and five arcades. The rood and parclose screens are 15th century with restoration by Herbert Read in 1901. The font, engraved with the arms of St Peter and St Paul, is also 15th century. On the outside of the church you can see the Devil's Door, left open at Baptism. The Devil was believed to then make his exit! In Tudor times the village was big and busy. In 1536 the tithes and advowson were seized by the crown. In 17th century the village had the anomaly of lords of the manor who were Catholics. The church fell into disrepair. Then in 1777 Rev. Andrew Tucker became vicar and had the ceiling replaced, bells recast and churchyard improved. In 1842 church and tower were covered in roughcast.

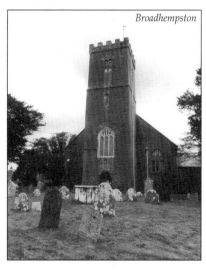

Broadhempston

In 1878 the chancel was restored, bells again rehung, a new oak altar and an organ were installed.

   Torbryan, Church of the Holy Trinity is a wonderful white vision in a special secluded spot. The Lord of the Manor, de Bryan gave his name to the hamlet. 'Tor Briane' means 'Briane`s hill'. He was a descendant of other de Bryans including Guy

Broadhempston to Torbryan

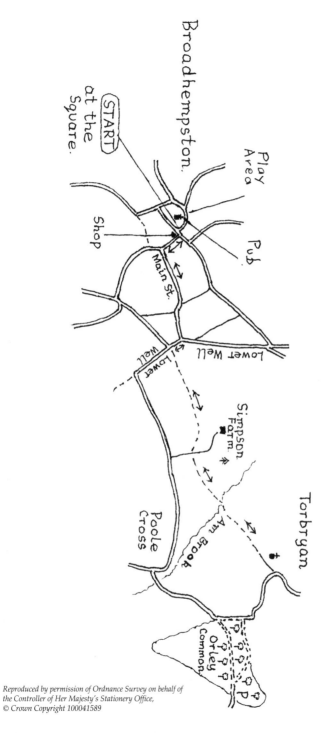

de Bryan who founded a collegiate chantry at Slapton in 1373. He was wealthy enough to have the church built all of apiece (1450 –1470) in Perpendicular splendour. The west tower in three stages is limewashed and overlooks the long low nave with its succession

Torbryan

of grand Perpendicular windows. The south porch has a fine fan vaulted ceiling. Inside, the church is light and white with arcades in light Beer stone. The clear windows also have some medieval stained glass. The wagon roof is white plaster with dark ribs. Box pews enclose the original benches. The long, lovely rood screen still has the original painted panels of saints and delicate openings. (We cannot approach too near as some thief stole 4 panels in 2003). We can gaze through to the perfection of the chancel east window and the interesting choice of Decorated style in the east windows of the aisles. There is much more of beauty in this church and all visitors are grateful to the Churches Conservation Trust for maintaining it and allowing us to enter despite the hazards of vandals. The then 'Redundant Churches Fund' took over in 1987.

The Walk
From Broadhempston Church cross the Square to the Community Shop and Post Office. Turn right and pass the shop on your right. Take the first turning to the left and walk down the main village street. You pass a variety of individual cottages and, half way down, another pub, The Coppa Dolla.

At the bottom you come to Lower Well at a T-junction and turn right. In 100 metres turn left into an enclosed path beside a pretty garden. The path soon opens to fields. It is well sign posted and heads northeast.

In 500 metres you cross a farm track. The handsome buildings of Simpson Farm are down on your left. Continue across fields and descend to cross Am Brook on a flat stone bridge. Hugging the hedge on your right, you now start the climb up to the hamlet of Torbryan.

First pass Old Church House Inn on your right and you see the Church over to the left.

To return to Broadhempston, *either retrace your steps over fields*

Or continue through Torbryan on the lane toward Ipplepen and Orley Common. Keep turning right on lanes for 1½ miles back to Broadhempston

Walk 8: Teignmouth to Bishopstone

This walk forges a way under and over modern roads to reach churches that must have been more accessible to pedestrians in Norman times
Starting Point: Tourist Information Centre, Teignmouth **GR**942727
Map: OS Explorer 110 **Terrain:** Seaside, riverside, gentle hilly lanes
Distance: 6 Miles

The Churches

St Michael`s Teignmouth stands next to the shore where once a solid Norman church faced waves of rough seas and invading enemies. A drawing of 1763 gives

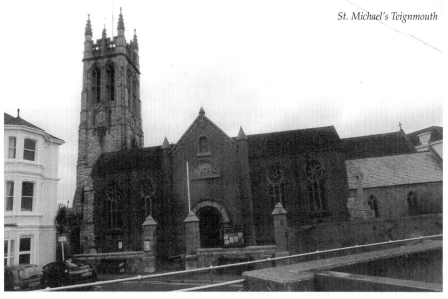

St. Michael's Teignmouth

a dramatic picture of a square tower and a round tower with cliffs behind. Affluent Victorian visitors to Teignmouth put an end to this scene. In its place they built a large conventional cruciform church with an imposing west tower. I could almost forgive them this trespass, when I entered to hear a harpist playing Victorian ballads.

St James the Less, Teignmouth was also a Norman Church. It has retained its square medieval tower in red sandstone. The rest was rebuilt in cream limestone in unusual octagonal shape in 1820. Both buildings make an impact in their separate ways; the octagon has a central lantern making it 8 feet higher than the tower. The two sections do not blend one with the other. The shape of the main body of the church may have the same basis as at Veryan in Cornwall: to allow no corners where

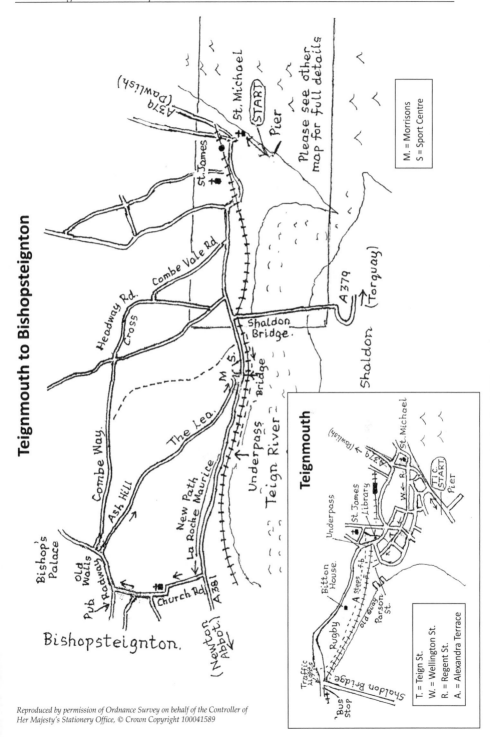

St. James the Less, Teignmouth

the Devil might lurk! Instead the church is encompassed with buildings and a maze of roads. Visitors who manage to enter will see cast iron pillars supporting a vaulted roof, tall slender windows and a medieval reredos. (Rectory phone 01626 774495)

St John The Baptist, Bishopsteignton on a Saxon site has good Norman remains. The font and the west doorway are Norman. The church is spacious with 5 bays and a north aisle. Outside on the south wall, a medieval treasure, revealed when the porch was removed, is the largest tympanum in Devon. It depicts the three Magi and Mary Mother of Jesus. Bishops have had a base nearby. Bishop Bronescombe built a Palace, now the Old Walls, in 13th century. Bishop Grandisson enlarged it in 14th century and also built a sanctuary chapel near the church for banished felons.

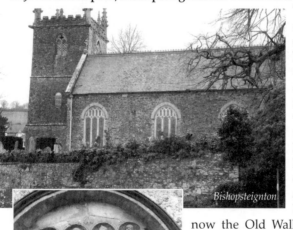

Bishopsteignton

The Walk

Note: Call at the Tourist Information Centre to find the progress or otherwise of a proposed cycle route by the river.

From TIC cross the Green to the Pier and turn left towards St Michael`s Church, a short seaside stroll. Turn left in front of the church and cross with care to Regent St leading to Wellington St, Bank St and Teign St. At the end you come to **the Quays** and note the dock entrance leading to 'Polly Steps'.

At very low tide it is possible for the intrepid to walk on the river side of the railway and cross a low wooden bridge over the stream, the Polly. You continue on rough shingle to walk under Shaldon Bridge and keep beside the railway until you find an escape route up to the main road to Bishopsteignton. In ¼ mile there is a bridge over the railway; in another ¼ mile or more there is a seedy underpass. Then climb low wide steps up to the road. Turn left and a pavement on the other side leads to a new footpath, 'La Roche Maurice' raising you above the road, A381. At Church Road, turn right.

From the Quays in Teignmouth there is an alternative route for high tide to

Teignmouth

Bishopstone. Turn right to find Parson Street which leads up past a funeral director`s to a covered metal footbridge over the railway. Once across, take the first turning left then go down a flight of steps to the road below. Walk in front of the houses of Alexandra Terrace until you come to the park behind Bitton House. Continue to the Rugby Field where the footpath is enclosed and then climbs up to Shaldon Bridge.

Turn right to traffic lights at a main road junction. Then turn left onto the road to Bishopstone. Almost immediately you come to a bus stop and might choose to catch a bus, Hop2 for the 1½ mile ride to Church Road, Bishopstone. Buses run every 20 minutes, less frequently on Sundays. *If you do not wish to wait, you can keep on course*

Teignmouth

to Morrison's. Go past the pedestrian way and take the main traffic entrance to the supermarket. Immediately, turn sharp left into an inconspicuous lane. It leads to Bishopsteignton, a distance of 1 mile. When you get there turn left for the Church. You then have to return on your lane or go down to catch a bus.

Low Tide or Hop2 Route: Climb up Church Road to a bend. The Church is on the right. (Do not forget to look for the tympanum on the outside).

Return to Teignmouth: Walk uphill past the Church to a Museum on the left and the Ring `O Bells pub opposite. Veer right toward the Old Walls Vineyard. Follow Radway up to crossroads.

The remains of a Bishop`s Palace at Old Walls is straight ahead.

Also ahead on the right, but not recommended, is Combe Way, a busier road back to Teignmouth. **Instead, follow this recommended route:**

At crossroads turn right into Ash Hill, a welcome 'no-through-road' sign means scarcely any traffic. *On the map it is shown as 'The Lea' and extends for over a mile.* It begins with a steep climb up to a bend and a sign to Park Farm. Continue on an elevated road between hedgerows with occasional gaps to allow views. After a bend the road descends towards the river. The tarmac is not so smooth here but still a good surface for walkers. Reluctantly come down to veer left to Morrison`s Supermarket where there is a café.

As you leave the store, turn left towards a sports centre. Turn right past Broadwater Estate and you come out on A381 and walk to traffic lights. Turn right to Shaldon Bridge and retrace your steps through Bitton Park to rail crossings.

Instead of going down to the Quays, keep straight on to find a pedestrian underpass below Exeter Road. It leads to the Public Library and St James Church is to the left. All downhill roads lead back to Teignmouth town..

Walk 9: Shaldon - St Nicholas, Ringmore - Stokeinteignhead

From a bright and breezy harbour town, find the original Parish Church beside the River Teign then climb to a village hidden in hills

Starting Point: Roadside parking, Picket Head Hill   **GR**933718
        Or Bus Stop on A379, Torquay Road, Shaldon **GR**932721
Map: OS Explorer 110   **Terrain:** Flat riverside then steep hills
Distance: 5 Miles + 2 Miles to include South West Coast Path
Local Information: 1. Bus 11 runs every 1½ hours between Teignmouth, Shaldon and Torquay. For times pick up the Teignbridge Area Timetable from TICs and Post Offices in Devon or phone traveline 0871 200 22 33
2. Shaldon is smaller and quieter than Teignmouth facing it across the estuary. It has good little shops and pretty stucco houses, some Georgian
3. Shaldon Bridge, once the longest wooden bridge, built 1825-7. It was rebuilt with 23 spans in 1930 in concrete and steel
4. Templer Way starts here but soon runs under water at High Tide so we climb up above the river.

The Churches
St Peter, Shaldon was open. For me this was its only virtue so I shall quote Pevsner who writes in praise: '1893 – 1902 by E.H. Sedding …A superlative example of Arts and Crafts inventiveness. Exterior of red sandstone and grey limestone striped. The long river front strong and uniform, firmly articulated by flying buttresses…Variety is provided at either end. Apsed chancel, north transept and low vestry; S.E. apsed chapel, W. front with a low baptistery between two lobbies, pierced buttresses, and a large west window with exuberantly imaginative flowing tracery, deeply recessed within a shady Gothic arch….' Concerts are held in this church.
    St Nicholas, Ringmore Road, the church I really wanted to visit, was closed. This 13th century chapel was the Parish Church until 19th century. The family of Stephen de Haccombe built the church in 1280. Over the years it has been enlarged and reduced according to fluctuations in population. Now Shaldon is bigger, and in 1894 E.H. Sedding modified this chapel. The east wall survives from the original church. It contains a little round window showing a leper receiving Holy Communion. North in the churchyard a grave inscribed 'Aturfuqil' commemorates the manufacturer of 'Liqufruta'.
    St Andrew, Stokeinteignhead has nestled in this sheltered village since 12th century when it consisted only of a nave and chancel. In 15th century aisles were added. The four bays have unusual pillars of red sandstone with capitals of Beer stone. Several saints, including St Andrew are carved in the capitals. The door is 600 years old. Medieval wagon roofs are impressive. The tower with stair turret is at the west end. The carved wooden screen is in Decorated style. The oldest brass (1375)

Shaldon - St. Nicholas, Ringmore Rd.
- Stokeinteignhead

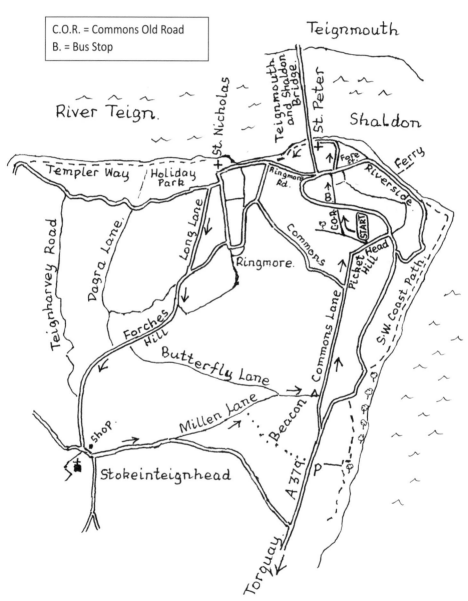

C.O.R. = Commons Old Road
B. = Bus Stop

Teignmouth

River Teign.

St. Nicholas

Teignmouth and Shaldon Bridge.

St. Peter

Shaldon

Templer Way

Holiday Park

Fore St.

Riverside

Ferry

Ringmore Rd.

B

C.O.R.

START

Teignharvey Road

Dagra Lane.

Long Lane

Ringmore.

Commons

Picket Head Hill

S.W. Coast Path

Forches Hill

Butterfly Lane

Commons Lane

Beacon

Millen Lane

Shop

A379.

P

Stokeinteignhead

Torquay

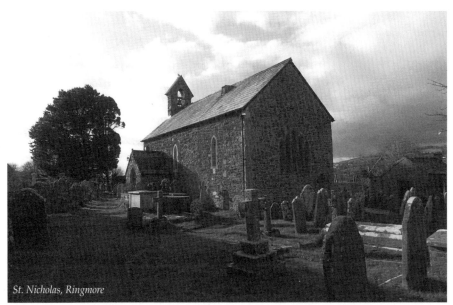

St. Nicholas, Ringmore

in Devon lies behind the altar rails. It is of a priest in vestments. Elizabeth Furlong is remembered in a brass in front of the pulpit. Her family owned the Manor of Gabwell. The original Church House has become the village inn.

The Walk

If you have parked near the seat on a ledge on Picket Head Hill, you will notice the wonderful view over Shaldon, river on one side and sea on the other. There is an unmarked track heading north through woodland. This is Commons Old Road. Follow it down to the A379 just outside Shaldon.

Cross this main road to the **bus stop** diagonally left opposite and over a grassy patch. Continue along Commons Old Road through a housing estate and down to Fore Street. This brings you past pretty houses and shops to Riverside. Turn left and walk towards Shaldon Bridge. Before you reach the bridge, you pass St Peter`s Church overlooking the River Teign.

Cross A379 again to Templer Way opposite, following the south side of the wide River Teign. Shaldon Bridge is on your right. You now have a spacious promenade and cycle track. You pass the garden entrance to a pub and come to a little lane, the Strand on the right. *Templer Way continues along the shore of the river and is under water at high tide.*

So revert to Ringmore Road and look out for the entrance to St Nicholas Church on the right.

From St Nicholas Church return to the Ringmore Road that curves past two beautiful white old houses, the Priory and the Hermitage.

After a bend to the right, take the second lane on the left. Long Lane climbs away from the river and past the hamlet of Ringmore on the left. In ½ mile avoid the

Shaldon

turning back to Ringmore on the left. Keep climbing and pass tracks to right and left. You are high on Porches Hill where a lone house surveys the coastal scenery. Pass Butterfly Lane, a track on your left.

Here is an escape route cutting out Stokeinteignhead (see the map).

To continue to Stokeinteignhead, keep to the tarmac road. Avoid Dagra Lane, a track on your right and start descending. In ½ mile, after passing another track, you come down into the valley where. the Church of St Andrew dominates the village. Turn left then right into Church Lane.

From Stokeinteignhead pass the village shop on your left. Immediately turn left into Deane Road.

In ¼ mile turn left again into a farmyard where the track, Millen Lane curves to the right then heads northeastwards steadily uphill for 1 mile. It takes you up through rich pastures and rolling countryside. Wild flowers on either side of the track give you an excuse to linger and regain your breath.

In about 1 kilometre I noticed that an unofficial path across the field on the right leads to the main road, A379. Walkers had obviously cut across to the Coast Path here. I did not take this route.

Shortly after this, Millen Lane is joined on the left by Butterfly Lane and the joint track leads past the Beacon to Commons Lane.

Turn left and head downhill all the way towards Shaldon. There are few houses on this road. In 1 kilometre avoid a road on the left and go more steeply down to the bend where a seat near the track, Commons Old Road guards your vehicle.

*This familiar track through the wood on the left leads to A379 Cross to the **bus stop** opposite for the 11 bus to Torquay.*

Walk 10: Coombe Cellars Pub to Haccombe and Combeinteignhead (Coffinswell)
an extension shown in brackets below

From a riverside pub climb along quiet lanes to a Manor House chapel, (continue to Norman village) and return on tracks via Combeinteignhead

Starting Point: Coombe Cellars Pub (park at end) south bank of River Teign **GR**902724
Map: OS Explorer 110   **Terrain:** Moderate Hills; some fields and hedgerows have been here in Norman times   **Distances:** 6 or 10 Miles
Local Information: 1. Coombe Cellars, overlooking the Teign, was renowned for smuggling in 19th Century
2. Haccombe House takes its name from the family who first held the manor in 12th century. It passed to the Courtenays in 13th then by marriage to the Carews in 15th century. The present early 19th century manor house in Georgian style has been converted into flats.

The Churches
Haccombe St Blaise is a medieval church packed with fine monuments, a tribute to past owners of the manor house. One is to Sir Stephen de Haccombe who probably founded the original church, built in 1233. In 1328 Bishop Grandisson dedicated the Church to St Blaise. In 1335 a college of six chantry priests was founded here and the Rector is still known as the 'Arch-priest'. The church was

Haccombe

Coombe Cellars - Netherton (Coffinswell) and Combeinteignhead

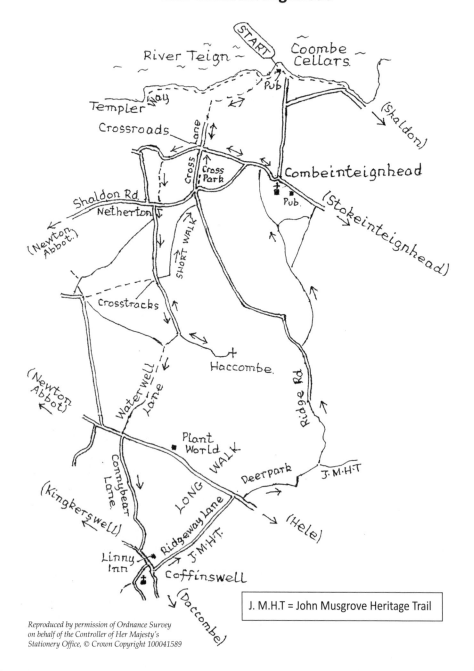

J. M.H.T = John Musgrove Heritage Trail

enlarged in 14th century. The north arcade cut through the outer wall. It has short octagonal piers. There are rare floor tiles and some medieval glass. The lancet windows contain roundels of Flemish glass. The screen, pulpit and reredos are carved in Georgian stone. The church is open on Wednesday afternoons and for Sunday services.

Coffinswell, St Bartholomew is in an ancient valley hamlet of cob and thatch cottages. The name is Anglo-Saxon. The Daccombe or Aller Brook leads down to the Teign. Near the church Court Martin is the 16th century manor house. The finely carved Norman font is the oldest treasure in the church. It is similar to that in Combeinteignhead. Nave and west tower are 13th century, south transept is 14th century, north aisle with 4 bay arcade is 15th century. The pillars have foliage capitals and the west pillar is unusual in displaying the coats of arms of the Holbeams (1473) and others. Some windows in the nave are 16th century. There are tall rounded arches to the tower and transept. Nineteenth century plumbers have left another unusual feature: their footprints on the tower screen.

Combeinteignhead, All Saints has a recent dedication (1986), as the original patron saint was unknown. It is known that in 1259 Bishop Bronescombe dedicated two altars. He may have noticed the 12th century font with round bowl and narrow band of carving. The only 13th century vestige is an Early English window in the

Combeinteignhead

east wall of the south transept. The rest of this cruciform church was built 13th –14th centuries. There are squints on either side of the chancel to enable those in the transepts to see the altar. The north transept has fine bench ends. They depict saints, including St Catharine and her Wheel and St Mary Magdalene and her ointment.

Other carvings are of grotesque animals. The Fokeray family of Buckland Barton had a chantry here. In 1887 the church was restored by Medley Fulford. He uncovered the rood loft and 14th century lancet windows but left a rather plain interior. The rood screen of 1450 was restored in 1905. Although the village is near the Teign, the name was not linked to the river. Instead it refers to the 'tyn hide' or ten hides of the parish.

The Walk

From Coombe Cellars Car Park, Climb up to the river wall, turn left and head westwards. *Templer Way continues beside the river.* You go down some steps to a field. You veer left and cross the field diagonally right. You join a track and turn left onto a tarmac road, 'Cross Park'.

At **crossroads** turn right to pass old orchards *where the local apple tree 'Netherton Pippit' still grows.* The road descends and bends right. You turn left to head south on a footpath past Orchard Cottage, through two fields and over a footbridge to the road at Netherton. Shaldon is to the left.

Turn right then immediately left on the road up to Haccombe, a distance of about 1 mile, the last part on the driveway of Haccombe House. On the way notice the cross tracks.

For the Short Walk, from Haccombe House retrace you steps to the cross tracks and turn right. The hedge-lined lane leads uphill. In ¼ mile avoid the path to the left. Instead veer right on the main track up to a tarmac lane. Turn left and you come down to the main Shaldon Road at crossways.

The road, 'Cross Park' is opposite. Follow this lane to familiar **crossroads**. Instead of returning to Coombe Cellars immediately, turn right and rejoin the Shaldon Road at Combeinteignhead. Keep on course to find the Church and and pub on a turning to the right.

For the Long Walk, from Haccombe House return down the driveway to the entrance. Turn left on the track heading uphill and southwest. This is Watermill Road. At a main road, cross to Connybear Lane which takes you down for 1 kilometre to the little village of Coffinswell.

From Coffinswell Church cross to Ridgeway Lane and follow John Musgrave Heritage Trail up to the main road at another crossing point. Continue on the Trail for ½ mile. The Trail veers right. You turn left into Ridge Road. In another ½ mile turn right into an unmade road down to Combeinteignhead. At the Shaldon Road turn right for the village centre. The church and pub are on a turning to the right.

Both Walks. From Combeinteignhead Church return to the main Shaldon Rd and turn left. Walk with care for ¼ mile as far as the lane on the right. It leads back to the **crossroads** where you turn right for Coombe Cellars.

3 Walks near Torquay

Walk 11: Anstey's Cove to Babbacombe and St Marychurch (Cliff railway)

A linear walk along a stretch of natural coast: bays, red cliffs, downland and woodland to the three giant churches at the northern end of Torbay.

Starting Point: Pay Car Park above Anstey`s Cove   **GR**936645
Map: OS Explorer 110   **Terrain:** Coastal slopes, sandy beaches and urban flat land
Distance: 4 – 5 miles
Local Information: Babbacombe Cliff Railway was built in 1926 to take holiday makers down and up from the Downs to Oddicombe Beach where they find a café, shop, water sports and toilets. Phone 01803 328750
Frequent buses **(32)** Torquay/ Babbacombe (traveline 0871 48 49 50)
Local chieftains Babba and Ansti may have given their names to the combes.
Notes: 1. Coastal erosion has caused some paths to be closed. Look out for Coast Path signs as cliff falls may have caused diversions.
2. The churches are firmly closed unless there is a service. The distant grandeur of these giants is their main attraction.

The Churches
Three large churches were built in a new Gothic High Church style in mid-Victorian times when it was fashionable to settle in Torbay
   All Saints, Cary Avenue, Babbacombe is a huge church in red sandstone with a tall white ornate tower. This proud design is by William Butterworth and considered

All Saints, Babbacombe

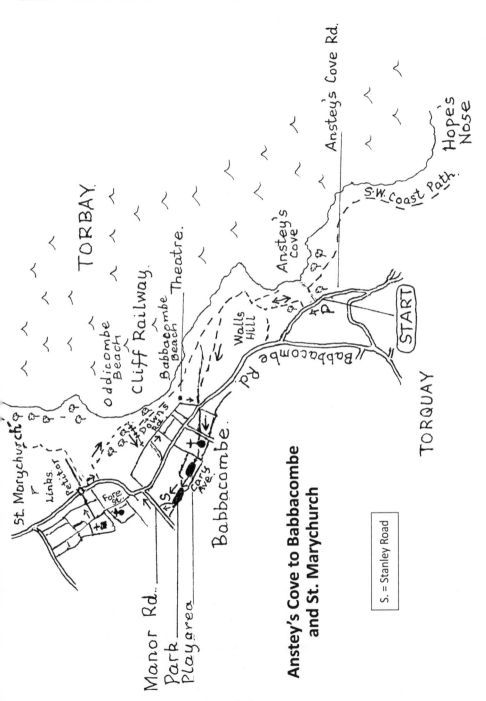

**Anstey's Cove to Babbacombe
and St. Marychurch**

S. = Stanley Road

one of his finest churches. The nave and aisles were complete by 1867. The chancel and tower came later, 1874. On the inside he has lavished colourful marble, not just 50 varieties of Devon but also Belgian and Sicilian. The short round piers are marble. The chancel, behind ornate brass gates, is dazzling with geometric patterns of marble including a carved frieze and brilliant east window. The bright glass in most windows is by A. Gibbs. The large chancel arch is echoed in arches into the aisles. The font and pulpit, both with double arcade carvings are in brilliant marble.

Services Sundays 9.30 and 10.30 and see notice board for Wednesdays.

Parish Priest Fr. Paul Jones Phone 01803 323002

Church of Our Lady and St Denis, Priory Road by Hansom, is another fine large church. The southwest tower has a spire and pinnacles. Inside there are

All Saints, Babbacombe

Church of Our Lady and St Denis,

ornate carvings. The nave is long; the north arcade lower than the south arcade. The gallery was built for the children of the nearby orphanage, now a school. Mass Sat. 6 p.m., Sun 10 a.m., 1st Fri. morning in the month, see notice board. Parish Priest Canon Michael Lock Phone 01803 327612

St Mary the Virgin, Fore Street is the old Parish Church for North of the Bay. An early Saxon church kept collapsing until, heeding the voice of Our Lady, the new building was sited on this hill. Bishop Leofric of Exeter held the Manor in 1050. Then, after the Norman Conquest Bishop Osborn took over. The Normans built a larger church. This survived until 1850 when it was demolished; the Norman tower was the last to go. It was replaced by the present 137 feet high tower, dedicated to Bishop Philpott. In 1943 the Church was bombed, killing 26 children and 3 teachers. Only the tower and the rood screen have survived from war damage. The body of the church was rebuilt 1952-6 in local grey limestone. The 12th century font has scenes of a man and dog, a man with sword, a dancing girl, a boar, and a harpist.

Masses: Mon. 9.30, Tues. 9, Weds. 7 p.m., Thurs. 1 p.m., Fri.9.30, Sat. 9.30
Sunday services: 8 and 10 a.m. and 6.30 p.m. Parish Office: 01803 327661

The Walk

From the Car Park, a steep walk down to Anstey`s Cove brings you to an idyllic view but limited access to the sea as the main beach is closed after erosion. Only walkers have access to the Cove. In May we had it to ourselves. The kiosk was just opening for summer season.

From Anstey`s Cove climb back to the Car Park and turn right on the road. You

Church of Our Lady and St Denis,

The Parish Church of St. Marychurch

enter woodland and soon turn right on the Coast Path. You have a steady climb through trees for nearly ½ mile.

Emerge to open downland above the wide sea on your right. *You can look back to the inaccessible rocks at the edge of Anstey's Cove.* Keep on course northwest. You are on Wall Hill, heading to Babbacombe where the first giant, All Saints overwhelms the town. The short Walls Hill Road takes you into Babbacombe.

Cross the main road with care diagonally right. Here a quieter back way, lined with terraced houses, St Anne's Road leads to All Saints Church. The main porch is on the other side. Sadly it is firmly locked. Return until you are opposite a grassy play area and a local sign to St Marychurch.

Go through the play area and continue to another green space, mainly used by dog walkers. Veer to the right and cross to Stanley Road leading to busy Manor Road. Turn right and walk on pavement past shops to cross roads. Turn left and walk to traffic-free Fore Street where you can linger among attractive individual shops including a private bookshop.

As you pass along Fore Street, look up a lane on the left to see the second giant, the Church of Our Lady and St Denis, also closed and locked.

Finally, near the end of Fore Street you come to the third giant, the dark grey Church of St Mary the Virgin, also closed and locked. As you go around the church looking in vain for an open door, you can look across to the second giant in light stone with a soaring tower.

From St Mary the Virgin return to Fore Street and turn left then immediately right. A side road leads to a small roundabout at the main road. Cross carefully to pavement on the other side. *Here the Coast Path has had to come inland along Petitor Road.* But we are heading south for our return.

Ignore Petitor Road and turn right to walk parallel to the main road. In 50 metres you can escape to a grassy space on the left. Follow the Coast Path signs to 'Babbacombe Bay'.

Veer right to walk steadily downhill on a lovely grassy swathe between trees. Enter the trees on your right and steps down and up lead beside the Babbacombe Cliff Railway. You are spared the need to keep climbing to the top, when a narrow underpass allows you to cross below the railway.

Turn left to go down to the tarmac lane to Oddicombe Bay below (see Local Information above). Here you can take the funicular train up to the promenade at Downs Road.

If you wish to continue on the Coast Path, you have to climb above the original route and head round the Bay to Car Parks at Beach Road and Walls Hill Road where you can climb up to Walls Hill.

For those who have opted for the rail up to Babbacombe Downs, turn left on the promenade, walk around past the Theatre and turn into the familiar Walls Hill Road.

Retrace your steps over the Downs and through the woods to Anstey's Cove.

Walk 12: Torre Abbey to Cockington

Oases in the conurbation of Torbay enable us to walk from a Norman Abbey to a Saxon village.

Starting Point: Torre Abbey, King`s Drive, Torquay   **GR**906637
The Car Park is behind the Abbey. **Torquay Station** is ¼ mile away.
Bus 62 links Torquay town centre with Torre Abbey and Cockington.
Map: OS Explorer OL20   **Terrain:** Mainly flat   **Distance:** 5 Miles
Cockington Village and Cockington Court are part of a quite extensive Saxon estate that has survived in the midst of later development. It is unspoilt and quite delightful. With trepidation I read that it is due for a grant. It is perfect as it is, free and informal and long may it stay so. The first village was called Cocca`s Tun. No doubt a stream in a fertile valley attracted the Saxon farmers. After the Norman Conquest the Fitzmartins took over as lords of the manor. Three hundred years later the influential Cary family owned the estate. In 1654 they were succeeded by the nouveau rich – the gold merchant Mallocks. In 18th century they converted the Tudor house into a three storey manor. The north side and kitchen of Cockington Court are still Tudor. Torbay Borough Council has maintained the estate as a beautiful park. The village has a mill, a forge, an inn and several thatched cottages, including tearooms. The Church and Big House are a walk away across the Park. They were open and full of life on our visit in May. We also enjoyed woodland, beautiful lakes and a dilapidated gamekeeper`s cottage.

The Churches

Torre Abbey grew to be the wealthiest Premonstratensian house in England.

Torre Abbey

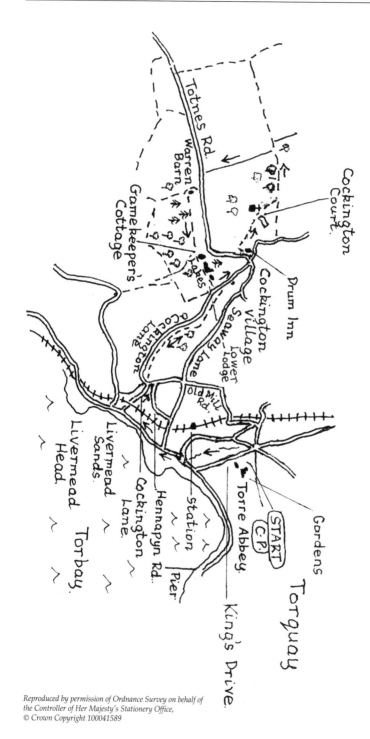

Torre Abbey to Cockington

William de Brewer founded the Abbey in1196 as a thanksgiving for the safe return of his son who had been a prisoner in Austria. After the Dissolution the building partly fell to decay. In 1598 Thomas Ridgeway made his home here. In1662 it became the private residence of the influential Cary family who were here for 300 years. In 1930s the local council bought the Abbey. Today the Heritage Lottery Fund has invested millions into restoring Torre Abbey to open in July 2013. There will be a history gallery and guided tours.

Phone 01803 293593

To the north **Torre Abbey Gardens** are on the Abbey cemetery. Remains of the Abbey Church, Lady Chapel and the Chapter House arch are on view.

The gardens are open from 10 a.m. to 4 p.m for a small charge.

Torre Abbey gardens

Cockington Church, St George and St Mary was built by the Normans in 1069. From 1203 Cannons of Torre Abbey held services and maintained the chapel. In mid 14th century it was enlarged. After the Reformation, the vicar was no longer a monk. It remained a private chapel until 1889 when it became the Parish Church. The tower of 1210 –30 is the oldest part. Its walls are 6 ft 3 inches thick. A cannon from Torre Abbey stayed in the upper chamber with a fireplace below. He had his office over the south porch via a gallery. The nave with north and south arcade is Perpendicular. The south arcade has a green man carved on the capital of the west pier. There is an intricately carved rood screen the width of the church, 42 feet. Originally 15th century it was skillfully restored 1916 – 20. The octagonal font was given by Robert Cary around 1485. Each side has a shield depicting families related by marriage to his family. Despite its remote place, the Church suffered much

Cockington

Cockington

damage by Cromwell`s men who broke the windows and other medieval treasures. The east window was again damaged in the war in 1943. The glass is now 20th century. Many weddings are held here in the charming parkland with the nearby cafe in Cockington Court.

The Walk

As you leave Torre Abbey turn left and cross the main road, King`s Drive to the strip of gardens opposite. Follow the stream through the gardens towards the sea front.

Turn right and walk along the sea front. The South West Coast Path shares the Torbay Road, A3022. Walk along the pavement for 500 metres towards Livermead Head. At Livermead Sands turn right into Cockington Lane,

Go under the railway bridge and past hotels. You soon come to a road junction and roundabout. Cross to the footpath diagonally right opposite.

It leads to Cockington Village. *Cockington Lane, hidden from view runs parallel on the left.* Walk beside a stream through water meadows on sturdy boards. Avoid the occasional paths to the lane on the left. Keep going on this peaceful path for 1 mile until you are compelled to turn to the road.

Keep on course along the lane passing thatched cottages, Home Farm and the Forge at crossroads in the centre of the village. Avoid the roads and cross to the footpath beside a tearoom. You pass the tearoom on your left and follow the track up towards the Drum Inn, a recent building, designed by Lutyens in 1936. Keep the inn at a distance on your right and come up to the spacious green of Cockington Park. Saunter up past the Cricket pitch to the idyllically sited big house and Church. *If you have leisure to explore the rooms upstairs and down of Cockington Court and enjoy the tearooms, you may be ready to continue.*

Walk on the lawns between the house and church. Pass a **craft centre** on the right. Veer left to cross a small field. Up in the far corner is a path junction. Turn left and head towards Manscombe Woods. Start climbing.

You have an elevated path beside woodland at the edge of the main park on your left and a field on your right. Follow the main path and avoid turnings to left and right. You come to a field, Dew Park. Follow the edge of this field. At a T-junction turn left towards Totnes Road. The path turns left again and runs parallel to the road for 75 metres.

Come out on Totnes Road with a good view down to Warren Barn and Manscombe Woods beyond. Walk down to the barn and turn left into a woodland track in the valley leading down to the Gamekeeper`s Cottage.

From here paths lead haphazardly past a succession of ponds overhung with prize trees, acer, magnolia also rhododendron, azaleas and bog plants.

When you can tear yourself away from these water gardens, join the nearby drive down under Lower Lodge and you come back to Cockington Lane. A footbridge over the stream enables you to rejoin the familiar path through water meadows. Turn right and return over the boards to the roundabout.

Cross diagonally left to Hennapyn Road for a different route back through houses towards Torquay Station.

Walk 13: Paignton to Churston
by Steam Train

From a seaside resort take a steam train to a quiet hamlet and return walking along the coast.

Starting Point: Queens Park Station, (built 1861), **Paignton**   GR590605
Map: OS Explorer OL 20   **Terrain:** A linear walk on lanes, fields, hills, seaside **Distances:**
3 ½ Miles train, 6 Miles walk *can be shorter*

Local Information: The main line terminus is on one side of the level crossing and the steam station, Queens Park is on the other, sea side.
Steam trains to Kingswear on the River Dart run all year apart from most of November, all December and early February. Phone 01803 555872
Viaducts along the way were built as part of the Torbay and Dartmouth Line, 9 arches at Hookhills and 4 at Broadsands. They tower over us on our walk.

The Churches
St John the Baptist, Paignton is a large medieval church with nave, chancel, embattled tower, north and south aisles, transepts and south porch. Underneath the chancel are the remains of the Saxon church. The chancel walls are Norman. The font of red sandstone is also Norman. Between 1450 and 1500 the aisles were heightened and the transepts added. The north transept is the Lady Chapel. The south transept is the beautiful Kirkham Chantry. Entry is through a carved stone screen with many images

St John the Baptist, Paignton

North door of Paignton Church

Paignton to Churston by Steam Train

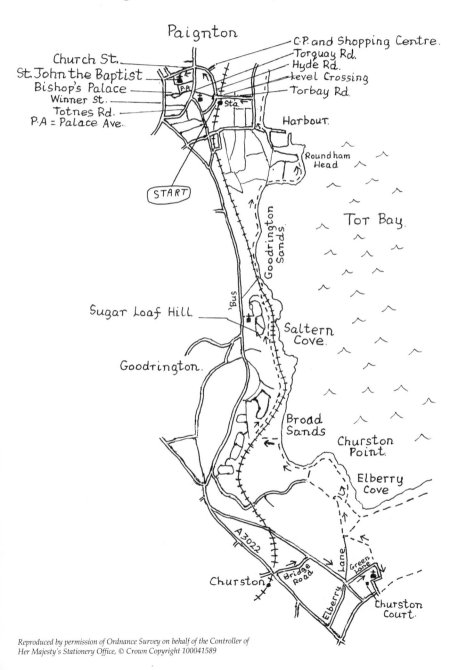

including the 12 Apostles, nearly all beheaded by puritans. Larger figures lying above on the tomb with a space under the arch are probably Nicholas and Jane Kirkham. The figures behind the altar are of Sir William and Lady Kirkham. They were recusants who refused to renounce the Church of Rome. A recess in the south aisle contains the figure of a corpse, complete with skull. The pulpit of richly carved Beer stone has survived, with a few knocks, from 15th century. You have to go outside the church on the north side to view the 14th century north door.

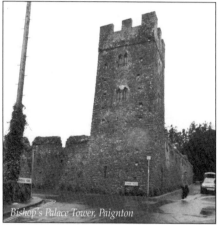

The lower part could be opened to eject dogs.

The Bishop`s Palace. From Saxon times until 1549 Paignton was an episcopal manor belonging to the Bishops of Exeter. All that remains of their palace is a walled enclosure south of the church with a tower in the southeast corner. Bishop Grandisson built the lower half in early 14th century and Bishop Lacy the top part around 1438.

St Mary the Virgin, Churston Ferrers was built as a manorial chapel. The south aisle was the extent of the Norman church. The plain tower dates from 1300. The

Bishop's Palace Tower, Paignton

tenants, the Ferrers gave their name to the manor. They also contributed to enlarging the church. They were followed by the Yarde family. Their seat was Churston Court, the Elizabethan house next door.. They had their arms and some animals carved on the capitals of the thin pillars. By 1480 the village owned the church. Much of its character of the 15th century church was lost in the restoration of 1850. In 1957 Agatha Christie gave the east window. Today, recitals are sometimes held here. Otherwise the church is closed unless there is a service (11 a.m. and 6 p.m. Sunday. Phone 01803 851570)

St. Mary the Virgin, Churston Ferrers

CARS
PARKED AT
OWNERS
RISK

The Walk

From Churston Station take the underpass to the other side of the busy A3022. Walk along Bridge Road to a T-junction. *The bridge here goes over a disused railway line. The entrance to Churston Golf Course is opposite*

Turn right and walk along the long, straight Bascombe Rd for ¼ mile, passing Elberry Lane. Turn left into Green Lane and pass houses on the left.

At the next T-junction, **note** the footpath to the left. Turn right, still on Green Lane, for the old hamlet, Churston Ferrers. The Church is to the right.

Just past the Church, Churston Court has been converted into a hotel and restaurant, retaining its old features.

From Churston Church return along Green Lane to the noted footpath on the bend. Here a track leads to the Golf Course. Yellow posts mark the line of the footpath across the Golf Course and into a coppice. Avoid the path on the right that delves into the coppice. Instead, cut through the edge of the coppice and turn right into an enclosed path heading towards the coast.

At the end of the enclosed path turn right then immediately left to come out on the expanse of Green looking towards the sea at Churston Point. Walk around the edge of the Green where two lines of seats have been spaced to take advantage of the view. We are on the South West Coast Path.

Seats were empty on our wet May day but we were rewarded with a glowering seascape.

Walk round Churston Point to the Bay at Broad Sands. Here beach huts overlook the sea. *The eye is drawn to the magnificent spectacle of a steam train passing high above green fields and across the viaducts (See above).*   Follow the curve of the bay to the last of the beach huts and turn left into a tarmac track. It brings you under the viaduct.

On the other side turn right and climb steps up above the level of the viaduct. For the next mile your path is now restricted between the railway on the right and houses or caravans on the left. There are flights of steps up Sugar Loaf Hill and down the other side.

If you are weary, there is a way out, just after Sugar Loaf, opposite a bridge over the railway line, turn left and wind your way to Barn Road and A379. St George`s modern Church is on the left and shops are on the right. Cross the main road to catch Bus 12 back to Paignton, it runs every 10 mins

To continue the walk along the Coast Path, keep on course beside the railway line for over ¼ mile when you come down to Goodrington Sands. Here you have a chance to walk along Promenade Paradise Walk!

The Coast Path goes round Roundham Head or you can cut through Vista Road and head for the Harbour. Join Eastern Esplanade as far as a cinema and café overlooking Paignton Sands. Turn left into Torbay Road leading back to Queens Park Station.

To continue to St John the Baptist, on the town side of the level crossing veer right and walk along Hyde Road, past shopping centre car parks to cross roads. Cross main Torquay Road to Church Street. The Church is up on the left. Turn left to enter the church. Keep on course southwards to visit the remains of the Bishop`s Palace.

4 Walks near Kingsbridge

Walk 14: West Charleton to Kingsbridge

A scenic estuary and town walk that includes three rather plain churches and rocky green lanes

Starting Point: The verge, Church Lane, West Charleton   **GR**749427
Map: OL20   **Terrain:** Hilly, some stony uneven tracks, damp crossing at head of estuary   **Distance:** 8 Miles (Could be shortened by catching a bus)
Local Information: Bus 93 (Dartmouth to Plymouth) calls at West Charleton Village Hall for passengers to Kingsbridge and beyond approx. hourly Monday to Saturday. For details phone 0845 6001420
 Charleton supplied fine slate for church building in 13th century. The square tower of Dartmouth Castle was built of Charleton slate in 1488. Many a local farm had a quarry. Goose Quarry was on a much larger scale.
The Ashburton Arms started life as a farm.
In 19th century, the Lords of the Manor were benevolent landlords. They lost their assets after World War 1 when Earl Compton broke his engagement to dancer, Daisy Markham. She sued and was awarded £50000. The estate broke up. Many tenants bought the homes they had previously rented.
Kingsbridge 'is a small town on a steep hill which rises from the head of a beautiful, many branched estuary. There was a bridge here in the 10th cent.' - W.G. Hoskins 1954. Today there are too many cars 2014.

The Churches
West Charleton, St Mary is built of the local slate. It stands high and slightly apart from the village. It is a grey austere building with a 14th century tower that would fit a castle. The austerity continues in the large barn-like interior. The old screen and rood loft have been removed. Sedilia and piscina are still there. In 1849 nave and aisles were rebuilt. There is a four-bay north arcade. The windows were restored in Decorated sryle. In 1970 the stained glass in the south transept window was installed. It shows Mary, Mother of Jesus.
   Kingsbridge, St Edmund King and Martyr takes its dedication from the King who found refuge in 869 under the arches of a bridge to escape the Danes. A chapel was founded here in 13th century by permission of the Rector of Churchstow. There is a central tower and spire that beckon sailors arriving up the estuary. In 15th century the church was enlarged with the addition of aisles and using some stones from the earlier chapel. The font was also retained. In 1414 Bishop Stafford of Exeter consecrated the church. Screens and porch are from this building. Parts of the rood screen have been used to make the pulpit and the reader`s desk. The parclose screen is unique. In 1849 a large chapel was added to the west of the south transept. Later that century the nave was rebuilt. .

West Charleton to Kingsbridge

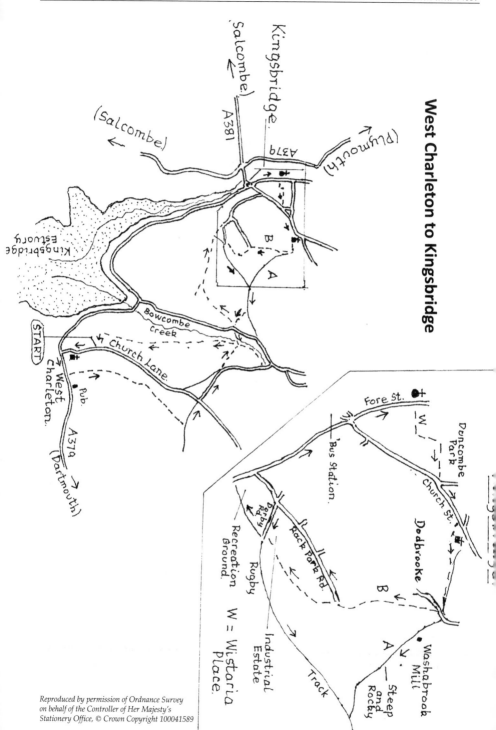

Kingsbridge

Dodbrooke, St Thomas of Canterbury stands in a separate medieval settlement that had its own market in 1257. There was probably a church here in 1220 and possibly earlier. One of the murderers of St Thomas a Becket if believed to have held land here. He was William de Tracey. The oldest parts of the present church are the

Dodbrooke

Perpendicular nave and
south aisle. The pillars of the
south arcade are monoliths.
Their capitals are more
ornate in the chancel. An
emblem of the Bishop of
Lacy, who died in in 1455,
can be seen on one capital.
Look for the Lacy Knot. The
rood screen has been
skillfully restored and there
is a fine parclose screen. The

Dodbrooke

porch is 15th century with an older inner doorway. The north aisle, once belonging
to the Champernownes of Dartington, was neglected. Edmund Sedding restored
the church 1878 – 1887. The north aisle was rebuilt using pillars from the ruin of
South Huish Church.

The Walk

*Church Lane was the only land route to Kingsbridge until the road across the estuary was
built in 19th century.*

Walk down Church Lane, passing St Mary`s on the left. Cross the main road, A379
to a footpath on the other side. This path enables you to walk beside the road,
screened from traffic, to the edge of West Charleton.

You have to walk on the road here but only few metres. When you see a footpath
sign on the right, cross over and turn left into an obscure narrow path down to a
driveway.

You have a glimpse of the Church to the left then an enclosed path with a stream
on the left. The path follows upstream for 1 mile. Shortly after passing The Grange,
high on the left, you cross the stream to walk up through meadows. Keep in the
valley of the stream and veer to the right, northeast. Elderly horses ignored us as
we walked up to a crosstrack.

Climb the stile over to the crosstrack and turn left to walk up to tarmac at
Duncombe Cross. *To the left is Church Lane and leads back to West Charleton. To the right
the lane leads to East Allington.* Avoid both and go straight on, passing a pair of solid
stone houses.

In ¼ mile you come to a footpath on the left and magnificent views over the
estuary. *If you have doubts about crossing on the path below, you can make a ½ mile detour
on the road. Turn left at Bowcombe Bridge. See Map.* Otherwise turn left into this scenic
path. Follow the hedge down on the right. You come to the head of Bowcombe
Creek.

Cross the flat stone footbridge to soggy ground. Do not be tempted on the path
to the right. Instead veer left through a gate and along a spongy walk to the road
on the other side of the creek.

Make for the footpath sign diagonally left opposite. It offers a choice. Fork left for a very steep climb to a field corner. Follow the fence on the left. Cross a slate stile into a wide elevated field and follow a hedge on the right. The path curves to the right. You are high above Kingsbridge Estuary. Do not be tempted down to the left. Keep on the top path until you come to a Rugby field.

Go straight on to the access road and cross diagonally right to a footpath. It plunges down a very steep grassy slope to the lane at the bottom. Turn left. *You can avoid this precipice by turning right on the road then sharp left.*

The lane leads past a small industrial complex to a recreation ground. Enter and walk past tennis courts and play areas to a café on the left.

You are next to the A379. Cross to the footpath opposite. Turn right and walk beside the estuary towards Kingsbridge town rising to its Church. First you come to the Quay and Tourist Information Centre.

Cross the Quay to Fore Street and walk uphill past shops to the Parish Church, set back on the left.

From Kingsbridge Church, cross Fore Street to an alley opposite, Wistaria Place. Go down past stone walls to a T-junction at the bottom. Turn left to a park. You have a view of St Thomas Church. Cross Duncombe Park and Bellevue Road to Church Street. Turn left. St Thomas is up on the right.

As you leave through the south porch of St Thomas Church, turn left and go through the cemetery to a traffic-free lane. Turn right and you come to a view of the countryside. You have a choice of routes:

Route A: *More direct but steep and rocky.* Avoid the first bridleway on the right. Go to the next bridleway leading down to Washabrook Mill. Pass the cottages here and continue to the steep rocky track straight ahead, southeast.

Route B: *½ mile further.* Take the first bridleway on the right and follow it along a platform above fields on the left. It comes to a housing estate. Keep on course along Rack Park Road*. At Derby Road turn left to the familiar industrial complex. * *It is also possible to turn left here ino the bridleway and go down a grassy slope to veer right to the industrial complex.* Take the green lane past the Rugby field but do not turn right. Instead keep climbing on the sunken rutted track, 'the green lane' uphill.

Both Routes unite high on Buttville Hill and continue eastwards. Avoid a path to the right. Eventually the track descends to the lane at the head of Bowcombe Creek. Turn right and walk along the lane to the familiar soggy path on the left. Retrace your sodden steps over the flat stone bridge.

On the other side of the creek, turn right *avoiding the earlier scenic path.* You still have fine views across the water. The new path follows the hedge on the right for ¼ mile beside the creek. It veers left and presents a steep stone stile. It then climbs diagonally left for ½ mile. After a sharp bend to the left it brings you to Church Lane above West Charleton. Turn right. for the grassy verge at the start of the walk.

Walk 15: Thurlestone to South Milton

From a church that looks out to sea, cross fields and lanes to a village and church 1 mile inland then back along the coast with sandy beaches.

Starting Point: Thurlestone Church (only 4 parking spaces so be prepared to pay in one of the seaside car parks).   **GR**673428   **Map:** OL20
Terrain: Hilly, quite rough under foot in places, 1 lane   **Distance:** 7 Miles
Local Information: These Saxon coastal villages were liable to attack by Vikings, sea storms and invaders from Ireland and France. '**Thurlestone**' is named after the prominent rock with a hole, washed by the sea. It was a Saxon boundary stone. **Bantham** was a Romano-British settlement and trading post. In more recent centuries smugglers brought their goods onto the sands and up the lanes.

The Churches
All Saints Church, Thurlestone was built in 13th century to replace an earlier church. The chancel with deep lancet windows, piscina and niches is of this period. The round Norman font in red sandstone with honeysuckle and zigzag no doubt came from the earlier church. The south aisle has Perpendicular windows and the grand south porch has battlements above a second storey. Look up to the boss depicting Elizabeth of York who married Henry V11. Smugglers are reputed to have hidden

Thurlestone

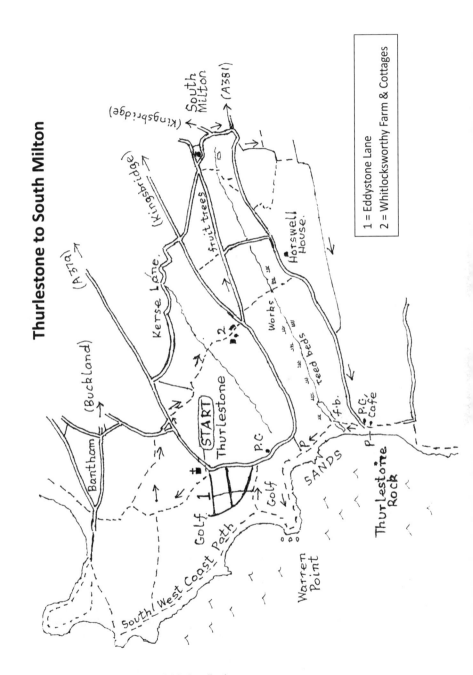

Thurlestone to South Milton

1 = Eddystone Lane
2 = Whitlocksworthy Farm & Cottages

their booty in the room above. The tall 15th century tower was used as a lighthouse. Particularly during the Spanish Armada a beacon is said to have glowed on top. The stair turret on the side is higher than the tower. There are no pinnacles. Inside the church, the stained glass is mainly by A.J. Davies (1920 – 30s). In the Lady Chapel a wall monument of 1658 has the figures of Thomas Stephens and family. The altar in this chapel is made of carved fragments of an old rood screen.

All Saints, South Milton stands on a slope above the Domesday village of 'Mideltone'. Much of the village is in a comb with waters that enter the sea. The first mention of a church here is 1269 when Bishop Branscombe licensed a chapel. Soon after his death in 1280, the church was enlarged. The chancel was extended eastwards. North and south transepts were added. Their two-light lancet windows

South Milton

and the squint are of that period. The south transept was restored as a chapel in 1962. In 14th century the west tower was added. Next the north aisle was built, absorbing the transept. The tower has pinnacles and a stair turret. The 15th century rood screen extends across the church. The screens were preserved in brown varnish by the Victorians and have more recently been restored to their old colours. Panels with many saints are revealed on the rood screen. The parclose screen is uniquely beautiful. Plain glass removed from east window has been used to fill other windows. The stained glass was installed in memory of Rhoda Far-Cox who died in 1935. The bronze crucifix on the east wall is dated 1150. The most curious and puzzling object in this

South Milton

South Milton

church is the ancient font. Its carvings, human, animal and devil or satyr hark back to Celtic times and have received many interpretations. There was a Druid grove nearby and perhaps an early Christian church.

The Walk

There is parking for 4 or 5 cars in the lane in front of Thurlestone Church. Stay on the lane to pass in front of the Church which you keep on your right. Avoid going straight on to Eddystone Lane and the coast. Instead, turn right at a finger post signed to Bantham and walk past the church on your right. The Golf Course is on your left. In just over ¼ mile, you pass a footpath turning to the left. Continue to the end of the golf course. You have reached the brow of the hill and turn right.

A short distance along the brow brings you to an enclosed footpath. Veer right here and go down past houses to the road to Buckland. Turn right away from Buckland and head down to the main road into Thurlestone.

Cross diagonally left to a footpath on a tarmac lane. In ¼ mile at the bottom, you are on an estate road. Turn left for a short walk along this road. Then turn right into a wide field. The footpath leads diagonally left across two fields and a concrete bridge over a stream.

On the other side keep to the right of the field and climb to a neglected yard. Turn right to the no-through-lane to Whitlocksworthy. Here there is a farm and several cottages. Turn left and walk up to a road junction.

Cross to the second lane to the left. It leads for 1 mile to South Milton. On the way you pass the track down to sewage works and also a fruit farm

You come to the Church at the top end of the village. After visiting South Milton Church, go down through occasional houses to a cul de sac at the bottom. Pass this on your right. Take the next road to the right, signposted to Milton Sands. Then take the second track on the left.

The track is steep, stony, rough and enclosed. Avoid the first path to the left in under ¼ mile. Instead take the second path in another short ¼ mile.

Turn left into an open sloping field. Keep to the boundary on the right and climb to join another track coming up from the left. Go straight on then immediately right on this new track. The grassy walls are not so high and there are some views below and behind to South Milton. Malborough spire can be seen to the left and the sea ahead. The track heads for 1 mile down towards the sea. It is a rough mile with a very uneven rocky surface. We forgot about the hardship when a small hare appeared and came right up to our walking boots.

Keep to the main track, avoiding all side paths. At the bottom the track turns right, passes a cottage and comes out on the same road to Milton Sands

Turn left and walk along the road for ½ mile to the sea. There is a café to the left and a view of Thurlestone Rock. To the right, just before the café, you can turn and cross the reed beds on a long wooden footbridge.

You are now in Thurlestone by the sea. Follow the Coast Path up past a car park and into the golfing area. Veer left for the walk along low cliffs to Warren Point. Then turn right and inland past gardens on the left and the golf course on the right. In ¼ mile you reach the main road, turn left and walk on the pavement up to Thurlestone Church on the left.

Note: *Strong walkers may want to continue along the Coast Path towards Bantham and the attached map shows other paths back to the Church.*

Walk 16: Ringmore to Kingston

Far from busy roads, we seek historic villages with thatched cottages, sheltered from the coast and we brave a small section of Coast Path.

Starting Point: Car Parks in Ringmore: opposite the Church   **GR**653459
National Trust Car Park ¼ Mile southwest   **GR**650450
Map: OL20 **Terrain:** Hilly, coastal and inland   **Distance:** 8 Miles + ½ to CP
Local Information:
**Journey`s End,** Ringmore once housed masons working on the Church 600 years ago. In the last century R.C. Sherriff stayed here and wrote his anti-war play 'Journey`s End', staged in 1928 to much acclaim
The Dolphin Inn, is 16th century, a perfect place in picturesque Kingston.
Many tracks from coast and village lead to 17th century **Okenbury Farm.**
Noddonmill is a ruined cottage, owned by James Taylor in 1850 when there was a watermill here. It probably supplied meal to Ringmore.

The Churches
All Hallows Church, Ringmore is a building added in 1240 to the south side of an existing Saxon Church. The north wall, now reconstructed, and the vestry are part of that first church, possibly built by Henna, Lord of the Manor of 'Reimore'. In 1354

Ringmore

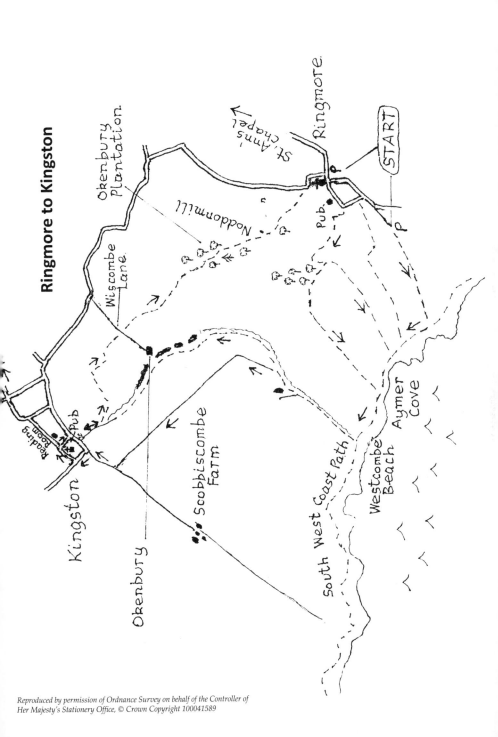

Ringmore to Kingston

the church was in a sorry state, due to the poverty of the villagers. Somehow money was found for repair work and also the addition of a tower on the south side. It is the only pre-Reformation tower in South Devon. The rector, a supporter of the King was hidden in the tower for 3 months during the Civil War. Lancet windows, some renewed, and containing modern glass are part of the 13th century building. The 13th century chancel arch has an unusual medieval painting in red, green and black above it. The screen was not added until 19th century. It was made in Belgium and picks out the colours of the mural. In 1862 Rev. Hingeston-Randolph had the church restored. He 'built out' the north wall, creating a tiny north aisle as Lady Chapel.

The Church of St James the Less, Kingston was originally attached to Ermington. Villagers had to carry their dead to be buried there in 14th century and the vicar walked over the hills to Kingston in 19th century! In 1402 the Pope gave permission for the churchyard at Kingston to be consecrated. The date of building of the first

church is unknown, possibly early 14th century. The chancel south window and the south porch are from this building. In 15th century it was enlarged with a north four bay aisle and granite piers. This aisle was in the care of Wonwell Court whose owners put in a wooden barrier screen and then neglected it. In 1824 the Archdeacon of Totnes ordered a church restoration. Windows had to be repaired and seats replaced. The vicar was responsible for the chancel but no-one repaired the Wonwell aisle until Mr H. B. Mildmay saw to it in 1905. He was a great benefactor giving land and a new organ. In 1891 the church was again restored and a 14th century window found in the west wall of the tower. Today the church fabric is flourishing and we can only imagine the past problems. Entry is through the north door.

Kingston

The Walk

Ringmore Church is at crossroads. The directions below are given from sitting in a car in the car park facing the Church.

Turn sharp left and head south-southwest for a good ¼ mile to NT Car Park You can postpone your visit to the Church and continue down to the sea.

For the walk from the car park facing the Church, turn half left and follow the lane westwards signed to 'Journey`s End', the pub. Go downhill to pass the pub on your right. The lane dwindles to a track and twists right then left, heading for the sea. After turning left you see a permissive path.

The permissive path on the right zigzags up through woodland then left high in the downs. Go straight on then veer left and follow the hedge on the right for a steady, sheltered path down to the sea. You reach the Coast Path at Aymer Cove. Turn right.

All routes. Turn right when you reach the Coast Path. *Walkers from National Trust CP have an extra kilometre of Coast Path to Aymer Cove.*

Walk with care along the Coast Path heading northwest. In ¼ mile after Aymer Cove you have a steep descent to Westcombe Beach.

At the bottom you will find a welcome path inland towards Kingston. It follows the course of a stream. Keep the stream on your right and in ½ mile you come to a newly planted willow bed. Here the path veers to the right and you have a choice of ways.

1. *Avoiding mud.* *The bridleway to the left leads up to a ridge and a long straight lane to Kingston. As you enter the village on the Scobbiscombe road take the first turning to the left and walk along the top road.*

2. In dry weather. Keep straight on along the lower Wiscombe bridle path. It passes a succession of lakes and a sewage works. It enters the village at a cottage at Walkspool. As you turn left into the village lane, **note** the path on the right for the return walk. Walk up the lane to a T-junction and turn left. Avoid a cul-de-sac Church Lane then turn right along the top road.

Both routes. The top road leads to a junction. Turn right for Kingston Church. Continue down veering to the right past the reading room to the pub, the Dolphin Inn. After the pub you come to a T-junction and turn right. Walk uphill to take the first turning to the left down to Walkspool. This lane is familiar to those who took the lower route to Kingston.

At the bottom pass the cottage and follow the footpath sign into the well kept garden and through a little coppice. You now have an easy walk across fields. Turn left and hug the hedge on the left as far as the field corner. Turn right then left on a zigzag course and passing Okenbury Farm below. You come to Wiscombe Lane access road to the farm. Turn left then immediately right to cross the lane and carry on along footpaths heading southeast.

You can see woodland, Okenbury Plantation ahead. When you reach the wood, turn right and follow it until you find a way through on the left. You have a straight steep path down through the wood. Gorse grows on the hill across the valley. Here there is a stream and plenty of mud. But it is a beautiful secluded valley. Walk above the stream on your left until you can come down to cross it at Noddonmill, a ruin on the other side.

Climb through trees. The track goes straight on but you turn right onto a steep footpath up the grassy slope. Find a gate into the final little field and cross diagonally left to the lane to Ringmore Church on the right.

Walk 17: Holbeton to Ermington

Following the course of the River Erme through woods and fields, we visit two grand Perpendicular churches in ancient villages, each served by a pub.

Starting Point: Village Hall, Holbeton   **GR**616503
Map: OL20   **Terrain:** Gentle hills, riverside   **Distance:** 8 - 9 Miles
Note: Flete Estate Office, 'Haze Farm', Holbeton, PL8 1JZ.
 To protect the flora and fauna by the river, permits are needed to walk through the estate from A379 to the edge of Holbeton. If you are unable to get permission, do not despair. Retrace your steps from Sequer's Bridge on public footpaths. In reverse the way appears different.
Filming: Countryside on the Flete Estate has appealed to film makers as a location for these films: 1978 'International Velvet', 1979 Penmarric, 1995 Sense and Sensibility (Jane Austen), 1997 Rebecca (Daphne du Maurier).
Flete is a Tudor house built by Hele. There have been many later modifications. The Hele family became extinct in 1716. The house is now a retirement home and some cottages on the estate are holiday homes.
Holbeton near the wooded banks of the River Erme and far from main roads is a pleasant, natural village of stone and thatched cottages.

The Churches
All Saints Church, Holbeton began as a Norman church and was extended in 13th century. There is Norman font with a square bowl. Bishop Grandisson dedicated the high altar in 1336. The Church dominates the village with its 15th century spire on an even older tower. It has a spacious interior with granite piers to five arcades.

Holbeton

Holbeton to Ermington

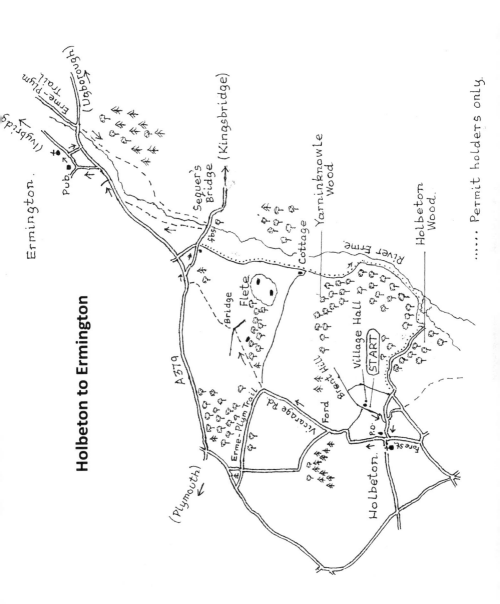

North and south transepts are quite short. The south porch has an impressive Tudor doorway. The Holbeton Church is fortunate in its 1886 Restoration by Sedding. Perpendicular window tracery has been renewed. Fine workmanship has also gone into the restoration of 16th century screens and benches. Wagon roofs were installed and some original bosses retained. Angels look down on the chancel. A beautifully carved stone pulpit and a grand marble font are all Victorian. There are monuments to the Hele family in the north chapel. Arthur Mee has likened this church to a cathedral. It contains much more of beauty and interest.

Ermington

St Peter`s and St Paul`s Church, Ermington dates back to Saxon times. In around the year 700, Saxons occupied Devon, making Ermington one of their hundreds. Edward the Confessor held the Manor. A wooden church probably stood here. The present building with tower is early 14th century. The steeple and Lady Chapel were added in 15th centtury. The steeple has a westward tilt but is not quite as twisted as that of Barnstaple. It was rebuilt in 19th century and the crooked shape retained. In 15th century the north and south transepts were developed into aisles. The arches are slightly higher where the transepts stood. The Jacobean screen has been restored by Sedding. He has not been quite as lavish here as at Holbeton. Instead, there are fine carvings of pulpit, reredos and bench ends by the Pinwill sisters. Their father was vicar here in 1880 and stayed for nearly 50 years.

Holbeton

The Walk

From the Village Hall, return on foot to the Church. On the way you pass almshouses then the post office and village shop. The church is opposite. Turn right at the post office and walk up Vicarage Hill towards Ford.

In ½ mile the lane crosses a stream and you are in the tiny hamlet of thatched cottages, Ford. Ignore the left fork and continue for another ½ mile to a junction. A track to the right leads to Flete House, not for us.

The long distance footpath, Erme Plym Trail approaches from the left. You follow it straight ahead northeast on a firm track through woodland and down to fields at Flete Park where Point to Point races are held. Pass their Offices on the right.

Keep on course for 1 kilometre along an unmade track that enters the shelter of trees on either side. Pass under a private overhead bridge. Towards the end, the track bends to the left. You go straight on over a stile and down across a field to the main road A379.

Cross the main road to a footpath opposite. Screened by a hedge it runs parallel to the main road. You have to cross a minor road to reach the River Erme. You are still on the Erme Plym Trail. Cross two wooden footbridges and turn left at the first footpath sign.

The trail divides so that it follows both banks of the river.

On the west bank you have a flat walk northwards across water meadows. In 1 kilometre, after passing water works, you come to the A3121. Turn right and walk for ¼ mile to the turning up the steep hill to Ermington.

The pub is facing you at crossroads. Turn right for the Church.

From Ermington Church retrace your steps across the green. Take the first road turning to the left. It bends to the right and goes down towards the main road. Just before you reach the road turn left to bungalows and cross a playing field to the corner on the right where you have access to the main road A3121 at a crossing of the River Erme.

Once you have crossed on the road bridge, turn right to join the other branch of Erme Plym Trail. There is a sign to Sequer`s Bridge, 1 mile away. First you have to squeeze between a house with garden and the river. Then you veer left uphill across a wide sloping meadow and into a smaller elevated field. Head for a conifer wood.

Inside the wood you have a narrow helter skelter path with glimpses through the trees of the river below. You soon emerge to flat meadows and a view to Sequer`s Bridge and A379.

Climb up to the main road. Turn right to cross the river. Look out for traffic on your left.

To retrace your steps to Holbeton, rejoin the earlier route across wooden footbridges and along the path screened by a hedge before crossing A379. You are on the familiar Erme Plym Trail heading southwest and only leave it when it takes a sharp right turn to the west after woodland. You keep heading southwest along lanes back through Ford to Holbeton.

If you have a permit to walk through Flete Estate, cross the road immediately after the bridge to the entrance and driveway. In ¼ mile you are below the House at a junction. Take the drive furthest to the left. It curves down below the House and quite near the river. You head southwards on this driveway for 2½ miles. On the way you pass a lone cottage and walk between woodland and the river. You are approaching the estuary and the river is spreading. You have to veer to the right and come out of the Flete Estate onto the Holbeton road. Turn right and walk along this quiet country lane. Holbeton Wood is on your left at first. The lane leaves the wood for farmland and enters the village from the east. Return to Holbeton Village Hall.

Flete

5 Walks Near Tavistock, including Dartmoor

Walk 18: Tavistock to Whitchurch
Tavistock to Shillamill

Two churches, linked to ancient abbeys, have come through the Dissolution and the Civil War surviving to serve the community today

Start: Tavistock Parish Church   **GR**482744   **Map:** OS Explorer 108
(a tiny portion of the walk continues on OL 28)
Terrain: a long slope up and down Whitchurch Down.   **Distance:** 4 Miles
Local Information: The Benedictine Abbey of St Mary and St Rumon was founded in 961 by Ordgar, Earl of Devon. His son Ordulph finished the building in 981 and then had to start again after a Viking attack.

The Churches

St Eustachius, Tavistock has historic links with the River Tavy and the Benedictine Abbey. The proximity of the river made this site ideal for the Abbey, built in 981. 'Tan Vechan' was the Saxon for River Tavy and the original name for Tavistock was

St. Eustachius, Tavistock

Tan Vechan Stoke. A church was here in 1268 but was replaced in 1318, thanks to Abbot Robert Champeaux. This new church was itself rebuilt in 1398 in the Perpendicular style we see today. In 1447 the Clothworkers` Aisle was added, donated by the widow of three wool merchants, Constance Coffyn. The pillars of this aisle have capitals carved with the badge of clothworkers: a two-leafed spray. St Eustachius is a spacious church in the centre of town. The nave has north and south aisles and five bays; the chancel has north and south chapels There are three large east windows, all with Victorian glass. The Mary Magdalene Chapel window

Tavistock to Whitchurch

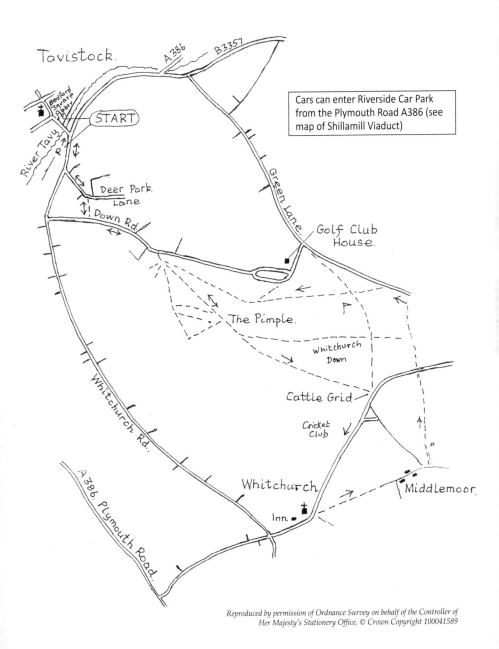

Cars can enter Riverside Car Park from the Plymouth Road A386 (see map of Shillamill Viaduct)

Tavistock to Shillamill Viaduct

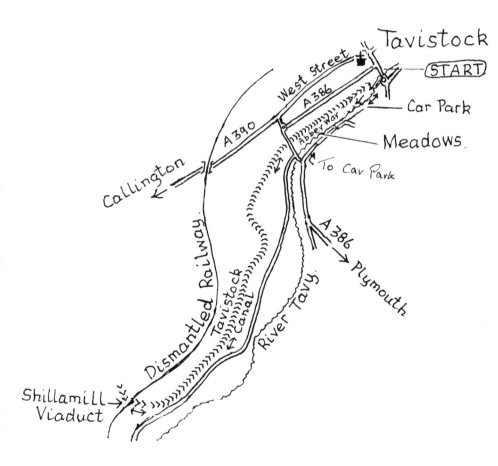

is the work of William Morris.

The wagon roofs have many bosses, including one depicting the three hares (see Widecombe Church, Walk 29). The tower once had open arches below to allow traffic through to the Abbey. The Abbey was dissolved in 1539 and only scattered remnants survive. In its place are Bedford Square and the walk to the river, Abbey Place, among other amenities.

St Andrew`s Whitchurch, on a more modest scale is also largely Perpendicular. The village of 'Wicerne' is in Domesday with no mention of a church. The first written record of 1288 observes a good income here. The Abbot of Tavistock planned

Whitchurch

to put a chantry at Whitchurch and claim the tithes. He died before this could be achieved. The Abbot of Buckland also wanted a share. He came for the induction of David Aliam as vicar. He had to retreat from the henchmen of Abbot Bonus of Tavistack. Bonus was dismissed but Tavistock kept the tithes until the Dissolution. Two local families, the Pengellys and the Sleemans bought the tithes. Some of their sons have been vicars here. Peter Sleeman (1848 – 70) kept a pack of hounds at the vicarage. The doorway and porch holy water stoup are the oldest parts of this church. The east window has original tracery, re-used in 1879 when there was a major restoration of the church. The chancel has a 14th century arch that was once above an Easter sepulchre. The slate panel is later, 1630. It has a carving of the Moringe family with a long row of kneeling children. The handsome carved medieval screen in the north aisle has come from Moretonhampstead Church. In the floor of the tower a gravestone to William Drake reminds us that his nephew, Francis Drake was a local man.

The Walk

From the Parish Church walk towards the River Tavy. On the way you pass the Information Centre on Bedford Square on the left and the Abbey Chapel, one of the surviving fragments, on the right.

Cross the river and turn right into the busy road to Whitchurch. Climb for 250 metres to turn left into residential Deer Park Lane. As the lane bends, you carry straight on in a cutting through to Down Road. You emerge to turn left then cross to the pavement on the other side. In another 300 metres you reach a wide cutting leading up to Whitchurch Down. Here you are on the edge of moorland where gorse abounds.

Follow the grassy way uphill on the left. Some select houses on the left back onto the Down. In half a mile you climb up to a prominent little stone hut, known locally as 'the Pimple'. From here you veer to the right.

First, you can sit and admire the views all around from three benches. Tavistock is below to the west and the hills of Cornwall are in the distance. To the north is the golf clubhouse and Dartmoor beyond. To the east is the golf course, crisscrossed with footpaths. Golfers, walkers, ponies, picnickers and dogs all seem to have free access to this blessed land.

Tavistock

Our route from 'the Pimple' is southeast, heading for a cattle grid 500 metres away. Locals can point you in the right direction. Otherwise, find a way on the edge of or through the gorse.

After the cattle grid and nearby finger post, turn right to the semi-rural road down to Whitchurch. You pass the Whitchurch Wayfarers Cricket Club on the right and reach St Andrew`s Church in 500 metres.

Monks used to stay at the Inn next to the Church. This Inn also served as a refuge from the storm. It has 12th century stonework at the back.

To return to Tavistock from Whitchurch, turn left from the Inn and look for a footpath on the bend opposite the Church. Turn right into a lovely elevated field under threat of conversion into a car park. Follow the well defined path northeast to Middlemoor and keep on course along a lane with mini stately homes on either side.

When you reach the Green follow the signed footpath on the left. back to the Down. You pass one lone house and follow the wall on the right. Keep on course, northwards, across the Golf Course.

You come to an open lane with occasional cars. Turn left and walk on the grass beside the lane and towards the Golf Clubhouse. Turn left and up towards 'the Pimple'. From here turn right and head back down, retracing your steps to Tavistock.

An Additional 3 Mile Walk to Shillamill Viaduct and back   Map: OL28
This walk remembers Victorian engineers who built the canal linking Tavistock with the River Tamar in 1803. In 1859 they made railways with huge viaducts - their work is done and is here just a source of leisure!

From Tavistock Parish Church walk to the River Tavy but do not cross the bridge.

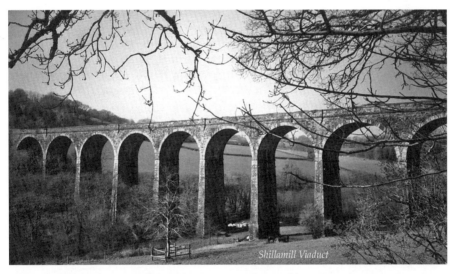
Shillamill Viaduct

Instead, turn right to walk beside the river along Abbey Way. In 300 metres you come to a recreation area, 'The Meadows'. Veer right towards the canal and join the tow path. Walk beside Tavistock Canal on your right. Go under the Plymouth Road and rejoin the canal tow path. It passes houses then playing field and workshops. It has become a wide, elevated track, lined with trees and passing through lovely countryside, a haven for birds. The river is below on the left. In 1 mile you reach the viaduct, a dramatic giant crossing above canal and rivers. The canal veers to the right and continues to Morwellham but we do not follow it there and must turn back.

Walk 19: Buckland Abbey to Milton Combe and Buckland Monachorum

This is an easy walk across fields and along lanes, allowing time to view angels making music and to explore the famous abbey

Starting Point: The Visitor Car Park, Buckland Abbey   **GR**489668

Map: OS Explorer 108 also OL 28   **Terrain:** One steep downhill, followed by a climb, otherwise gentle slopes or flat   **Distance:** 5 miles

Local Information: Buckland Abbey (National Trust) open daily at 11 a.m.
Closed from late December, all January and early February
Weekend opening only, late Feb and early March also Nov. and early Dec.
 For details Phone 01822 853607
The Garden House, Buckland Monachorum is open 1st Mar – 4th Nov
With formal and informal gardens and tea rooms.   Phone 01822 854769

The Churches

Buckland Abbey has undergone dramatic changes since Cistercian monks in white robes came here to settle and live a simple life of worship and self sufficiency, growing herbs and farming fish. They built the Abbey with its grand church around 1270. They grew to be rich landowners who could levy tithes from the farmers. Their huge tithe barn still stands, a marvel to modern visitors. Henry V111 must have delighted in

Buckland Abbey

Buckland Abbey to Milton Combe and Buckland Monachorum

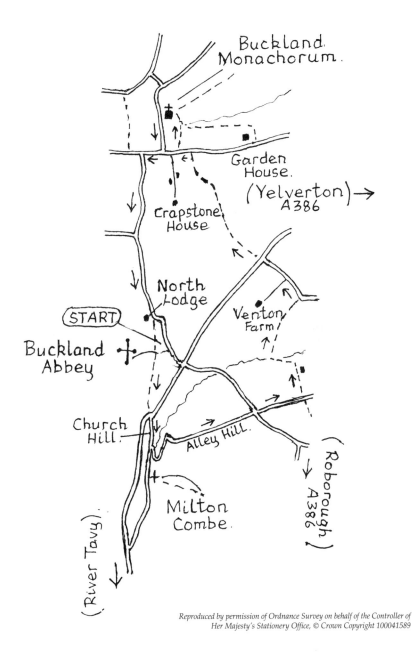

Reproduced by permission of Ordnance Survey on behalf of the Controller of Her Majesty's Stationery Office, © Crown Copyright 100041589

seizing their estate. He sold it to Richard Grenville in 1541. Thirty years later grandson, Richard Grenville, the bucaneer inherited Buckland Abbey and decided to convert the church into a three storey house. This conversion drained his resources and he had to sell the place to another sailor, his cousin, Francis Drake. Drake already had 40 properties. The Drakes lived here until 1940.

Tithe Barn, Buckland Abbey

Over the years they made further, less dramatic changes and finally handed the estate over to the National Trust – a happy ending! The 14th century refectory is now a restaurant. There are estate walks of varying lengths through fields and woods and down to the River Tavy.

Buckland Monachorum, St Andrew originally had a Saxon church and still has a Saxon font, a plain heavy structure. In 1350 a stone cruciform building replaced its wooden predecessor. Finally in around 1490 the old stone was used to build a handsome church with many pinnacles and large windows. From the beams of the nave there are angels playing a variety of musical instruments. The old font was hidden under the church and replaced with a 'modern' octagonal one. In 17th century the chancel was extended and given a wagon

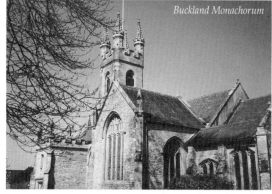
Buckland Monachorum

roof. The south chapel was also restored then. The chancel arch was raised and is now lopsided. Francis Drake (1540 – 96) saw nothing strange in leaving his desecrated abbey to worship in this neighbouring church. The south or 'Drake' chapel contains several large monuments by the sculptors John Bacon, father and son. The 5-light east window reveals the influence of William Morris and Burne-Jones. It depicts the four Evangelists and also contains fragments of old glass. The west window by Charles Kempe has his wheatsheaf trademark. The tall slender tower was weakened by bell ringing and had to be repaired in 1785 and again in 1980. Keen bell ringers practised all night in 1813 and were dismissed.

The Walk

From the Visitor Car Park, walk towards Buckland Abbey and turn left in about 50 metres. Here is a signed footpath leading out of trees into a field. You are heading south for ¼ mile towards the road. Just before the road, veer to the right on a short pedestrian cut.

Milton Combe

At the road cross to the lane opposite for a steep descent into Milton Combe. As soon as you reach the village in a hollow, turn sharp left to pass the pub, 'Who'd have thought it Inn' on the left. *If you wish to see the church, continue south through the village for ¼ mile*

After the pub turn sharp right then left on a narrow lane that leads out of the village on the other side. You head northeast on this rural lane for ½ mile to crossroads.

Cross to the lane opposite signposted to Horrabridge and keep on course. In under ¼ mile turn left into the field at a signed footpath. Follow the hedge on your right and walk down past Broom House to a stile in the bottom corner.

In the next field you have a fine view; a stream running along the valley and a slope up to Ventor Farm, a picture of stone buildings. Cross diagonally left down to the farm track that goes over the stream.

On the other side, follow the track to go through a gap in the hedge and veer to the right. Here is another hedge. With the farm on your left and the hedge on your right, climb to the top right hand corner. Go through the farm gate to the tarmac lane. Turn left.

Walk along the lane, past the farm that presents a more workaday face with huge barns here. In over ¼ mile you come to the road again at a more northerly point.

Cross to the footpath opposite. Go through the farm gate and walk beside the hedge on the left. You are heading northwest over a wide, flat field. In 1 kilometre cross to the other side of the hedge and continue over a smaller field. Pass the stone buildings of Crapstone House away to the left.

You come out on the road that passes by Buckland Monachorum. Turn left then in 50 metres turn right into a small field overlooking the village. Go down to cross a stream at the bottom and an enclosed path. At T-junction turn left for the church.

From Buckland Monachorum Church turn left and pass the pub on the left. Climb up through the High Street to the bypass road again at the top. Turn right. In ¼ mile turn left into the lane signposted to Buckland Abbey.

You are heading due south with ample verges and a fairly quiet approach. You may catch a view down to the Tavy on the right. In 1 mile you pass North Lodge then in 50 metres turn right into the footpath through trees on the Buckland estate. Cross a private track and keep straight on to the familiar entrance track Turn right to visit the Abbey. Turn left for the car park.

Walk 20: Brent Tor to Lydford including the Gorge and North Brentor

This walk has everything – historic churches, dramatic scenery, moorland paths, idyllic farms, tearooms, and flexible distances.

Starting Point: Car Park for Brent Tor   GR469805   **Map:** OS Explorer 112
Terrain: Hilly with some gentle slopes, steep and rough paths in the Gorge
Distances: 9 miles to but not including Lydford Gorge
                 5 miles to North Brentor
                 12 miles including North Brentor and Lydford Gorge

Local Information: Lydford was the most westerly burh or fortified town on the edge of the Wessex of King Alfred (871–901). He boosted its fortifications against the Danes. Vikings later destroyed Lydford Church then Tavistock Abbey. Both were immediately rebuilt. In the reign of Edward the Martyr (975-978) Lydford was privileged to have one of four mints in Devon. Locally mined silver made Lydford pennies until 1050. Some surviving pennies are in Castle Inn.

The Norman Fort built on the northwest corner of the Saxon town, Lydford

The Medieval Castle reminds us that Lydford was an administrative centre of Dartford Forest. Dartford miners held stannary courts here from 13th century. The castle became renowned for its jail and cruel oppression.

Lydford Gorge is a natural steep sided valley where the River Lyd has carved a way through rock. The National Trust has maintained pathways through this gorge mainly under trees. In places they are slippery and very steep. The rope handrails help maintain balance. Tea rooms are welcome at both entrances to the gorge. Phone 01822 820320 for details.

The Gubbins were a tribe of outlaws who used to live in the Gorge. Many tales have been told about them.

Westward Ho! by Charles Kingsley has chapters set in this part of Devon.

The Churches

The Parish Church of St Petroc, Lydford. There was probably a church here in Celtic times, as the dedication suggests. St Petroc established a Priory at Bodmin in 6th Century (see *Cornwall Walks to Churches*, page 36). If there was a wooden Saxon church, it may have held the Hurdwick stone tub-shaped font that still survives. The church was rebuilt in 1237 and again in 1261. Early English remains are a lancet window in the north wall of the chancel and the piscina. There is old masonry in the west wall of the nave also. The church was enlarged 1428 – 87 in Perpendicular style. The tower, built of huge granite blocks with a neck joining it to the church, the south aisle and porch were added then. The north aisle, in a similar style came later, 1887. Later still (1923 – 6) are the benches with ends carved by Herbert Read. The chancel screen also belies its appearance; it is not 15th century, but was made to a design of Bligh Bond by the Misses Pinwell in 1904. The southwest window

Brent Tor to North Brentor
and Lydford

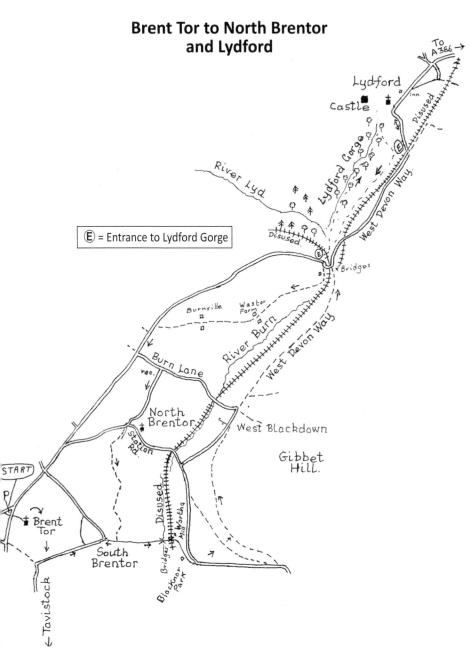

Ⓔ = Entrance to Lydford Gorge

Lydford

contains 15th century Flemish glass depicting St Catharine and St Anne. Mourners made long treks across the moors to bury their dead at Lydford Church. One route is known as 'the Lychway'.

St Michael of the Rock, Brent Tor – 'Is there anywhere in England a church more romantically poised than this, which has climbed 1130 feet towards heaven and settled like another rock on the top peak of Bren Tor?' Visitors come to this spectacular site on top of a conical hill, surrounded by Iron Age earthworks. It is believed that the first church was built here by Robert Gifford in 1130. His son, Walter asked for advice on church services. It was decided that the Abbot of Tavistock should supply two secular priests and a clerk to pray for the Giffords and other parishioners. The revenues would go to the Abbey. In 1265

Brent Tor

Bishop of Exeter, Walter Bronescombe seized the revenues of Brent Tor and some other churches. At the Dissolution in 1539, Brent Tor was one of the possessions together with the Abbey, given to John, Lord Russell. In 1912 patronage went to Exeter. The church today with north and south doorways is mainly 14th century. It is long and sturdy. The low walls are 3 feet thick, built of Spilite a vocanic stone. The south window with curved head may be 12th century. The narrow north window may be part of the original church. The plain octagonal font still has the clasps to fasten over the bowl to prevent the theft of holy water for black magic. The 15th

century tower has internal holes to allow drainage. The sundial on the south side has the date 1694. The stained glass was added to the east window in 1971. The church roof was rebuilt in the Restoration of 1889-90. Services are held in the Church in the summer.

Christ Church, North Brentor nestles in this hamlet as if it had always been there. In fact it is a mid-Victorian building with lancet windows and embattled west tower. Richard Gosling of Torquay was the architect.

The Walk

From the Car Park climb up towards the north side of the church. Before the top go round to the south side and through a gate onto a permissive path, following the hedge on the left. It leads down to a quiet lane.

On the right Holyeat Farm is probably the site of St Michael`s Well. However, we turn left and walk for ½ mile to South Brentor, a scattering of cottages.

At crossways keep straight on until you come to a sharp bend in the lane. Fork right into a track so that you can continue on your easterly course. In 100 metres pass a footpath on your left.

On the return walk we shall be emerging from North Brentor on this path. Meanwhile stick to the track towards a 'Weak Bridge' ahead. This is at Wortha Mill where there are two bridges to cross, one over the River Burn and one over the old railway.

After crossing the bridges, climb up the driveway past Blacknor Park, a large house on the right. Keep going above the house. Avoid the track on the left. You come to a moorland road.

Cross to the moors immediately opposite where ponies and people have made a wide grassy track uphill through gorse. In 300 metres of climbing you come to the first cross track. Go straight over. In another 150 metres you arrive at the next cross track and turn left.

You have a wide open path riding northwestwards on the edge of Dartmoor along the delightful West Devon Way. You can look across the road on the left over to North Brentor. *If you wish to shorten the walk to 5 miles, turn left and make for this village then follow instructions below.**

To continue the full walk, keep heading northeast on the edge of the moor, even when the road comes to join you. In another mile your track is fringed with gorse.

On the left you pass woodland and the peak of Was Tor rising above it. Step over the streams and water sources before veering to the left when you see a white cottage. You have reached Lydford Junction.

Cross two railway bridges then look sharp left towards an <u>old railway</u> approach. **This is the way back to Brent Tor.**

Before deciding whether to return, you may wish to enjoy the tearooms of Lydford Gorge. They are just across the way near the car park.

To walk through the Gorge to Lydford Church go to the nearby south or 'Waterfall Entrance'. Follow the designated route down to the waterfall then walk beside the River Lyd and follow the signs up to the Main Entrance where another tearoom awaits you. From the Main Entrance walk to the road and turn left for Lydford - the Church, the Castle and the Inn.

Lydford Gorge

From **Lydford Church** return through the Main Entrance to the Gorge. As you enter the trees, turn left to continue your circuit and follow the signs to the 'Waterfall Entrance'. Here you leave the Gorge and cross to the familiar <u>old railway approach</u>.

From **Lydford Junction** walk down towards the old railway line. **Stop!** In 75 metres you reach a driveway on the right towards a converted chapel. Turn right and follow the driveway as it turns left to go behind houses.

The driveway takes a southwesterly course towards Wastor Farm and an idyllic avenue, strewn with flowers. The farm enjoys wide views across to Dartmoor. Pass between the farm on the left and holiday cottages on the right.

As you leave the farm you have a short climb up to the footpath which continues on the other side. Turn right and go towards the steps on the right. Do not mount them. Instead, turn left to climb to a gate. Go through to a narrow footpath hemmed with briars. Luckily it is short and you are soon heading south over grassy fields. Keep to the stone wall on the left and do not be tempted to change course until you spy Burnville Farm ahead and may have to veer right.

Once again the footpath goes between farm buildings, this time along a farm lane. The main house is on the left and the coach house on the right. Walk along another tree-lined driveway. In ¼ mile you come to the road.

Turn left to walk down on the verge for ¼ mile, avoiding paths to the right. Turn left at the sign to North Brentor. Here the lane leads southeastwards past the recreation field on the right. At the first opportunity turn right to follow the village lane. The rec. field is still on your right. In under ½ mile the road curves through cottages and down to the village centre. Here at a junction is a bus shelter, a war memorial and a seat with a view to the church

***From North Brentor Church** walk to the war memorial and turn sharp left into a narrow village lane. There is a converted chapel up on the right. At the end of the lane a track leads into fields. Take the left fork. You have to cross a succession of fields in a mainly southerly direction for ½ mile. Look out for arrows on gates and avoid climbing to the right until you have passed a patch of gorse. You then veer up to your right and make for the left hand corner of the field to find an enclosed track.

This track leads to South Brentor on the familiar path in italics of the outward walk. Turn right and retrace your steps to Brent Tor.

Walk 21: Higher Dunstone to Widecombe

Cross the moors from a humble chapel to a 'Cathedral'. 'Widecombe has one of the best Dartmoor skylines, with huge boulders and outcrops of bare rock all round. Those who wander on the moors hereabouts will come across traces of its inhabitants in prehistoric days, Hut circles, pounds, cairns, kistvaens, and two strange rocking stones called logans.' – A. Mee.

Starting Point: Higher Dunstone Chapel   **GR**714757   **Map:** OL28
Terrain: Climb up to and down from moorland + 1 km on road.
Warning: It is very easy to get lost on the moors. Choose a fine clear day and study the map before you start.   **Distance:** 4 Miles

The Churches

Widecombe, St Pancras, known as the 'Cathedral of the Moors' is the focal point for small, scattered communities on Dartmoor. Widecombe itself is a small grey village in a dip in the stark moorland hills. The church is a long, low building mainly 14th century. The transepts were converted into aisles in 15th century. The

Widecombe

Widecombe

tower, by contrast, is tall and commanding. It is believed to have been built by tinners in 16th century as a thanksgiving. It is 135 feet high, all granite and late Perpendicular. There are 8 bells. Inside, the church has a simple majesty. The west end of the nave is clear of chairs, giving space. The pillars are monoliths, cut out of single blocks of stone. The surviving lower part of the carved screen has panels depicting saints. The many roof bosses could be the subject of hours of study. In particular, the three hares chasing each other in a circle. See also Braunton Church. **Higher Dunstone Methodist Chapel** was built in 1833. Its plain, dull, rendered side is on view. The other, handsome stone side faces the field. Dunstone was a Domesday manor.

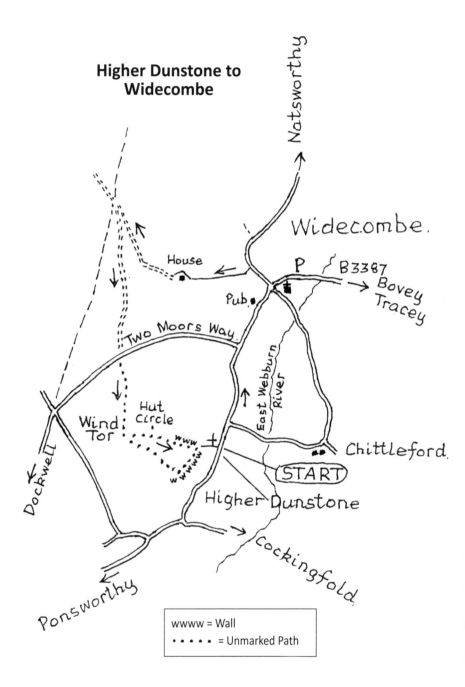

Higher Dunstone to Widecombe

wwww = Wall

••••• = Unmarked Path

Higher Dunstone

The Walk

With your back to the chapel, turn left and walk along the road to Widecombe, a distance of about 1 kilometre. Pass the pub on your left and the National Trust Information Centre and Church on your right. Keep straight on past the village green on your right. Your quiet lane curves to the left.

Ponies on Dartmoor

In 150 metres at a fingerpost, turn left into a rough tarmac track. It leads westwards, steeply uphill. *Turn to admire the view behind to Widecombe.* Ahead is a lone, stone house. You have to leave the track to make a detour. Follow the path to the right. It crosses a small field diagonally to the far corner. Here is a stile with a platform and a little stream below. You then veer left, still uphill so that you pass behind the house with its little woodland screen. Cross another stile then continue up to open moorland.

You come to a turf path, a long wide swathe worn by many feet traversing the moors. Turn left and follow this clear way southwards. *On the left you can look over Widecombe to the hills where Top Tor and Pil Tor rise.*

All too soon in 1 kilometre, you come to a tarmac lane.

If you want to play it safe, walk down this lane back towards Widecombe. At the bottom turn right. Retrace your steps along the road to Higher Dunstone

For a moorland adventure, cross the lane to the unmarked path opposite. Start climbing again. Veer left and head for 500 metres to the highest point. This is Wind Tor. The stones here are not very conspicuous.

Look back to make sure you know the position of the road you crossed. You may have to wait for a vehicle to show you the road.

Turn left and walk downhill in an easterly direction. There are several indistinct paths. You may, if lucky, pass the hut circle, again inconspicuous. In about 350 metres you come down to a stone wall. Look for a wall corner. Follow the wall down to Higher Dunstone.

There are in fact two widely spaced walls, each with its attendant path down to this hamlet (See John`s Map).

Walk 22: North Bovey over Easdon Tor to Manaton

A moorland hill separates two Dartmoor villages with their granite churches

Starting Point: Village Car Park, North Bovey   **GR**740838   **Map: OL**28
Terrain: Tracks up to high remote moorland then down to narrow lanes and paths through woodland   **Distance:** 7 Miles
Local Information: 1. Prehistoric hut circles abound on Easdon. To the west Grimspound has a circular enclosure with 24 Bronze Age hut circles.
2. Langstone was a Domesday manor.
3. Wingstone near Manaton was John Galsworthy`s home for several years.
Note: There is open access on the wilds of Easdon Down and few footpath signs. You need good visibility, fine weather and the aid of a compass.

The Churches

North Bovey, St John the Baptist stands in a leafy village overlooking the River Bovey. Built of moorland granite, the church is wide and low inside with five bays. Aisles, nave and chancel have ceiled wagon roofs. Their carved bosses are of particular interest in the 13th century chancel. One boss is of three rabbits, their ears meeting to form a triangle. Most of the church including the oak rood screen is 15th century. The figures carved on the entrance arch are similar to those of Manaton.

  Manaton, St Winifred was built in 15th century in Perpendicular style. The tower, two storey porch and south side have castelling. In 1779 a storm damaged the

North Bovey

tower and nave and glass windows shattered. Repairs and restoration have been ongoing. The 11 bay rood screen has survived despite damage during the Reformation and has been well restored by Anna

Manaton

North Bovey - Easdon Tor - Manaton

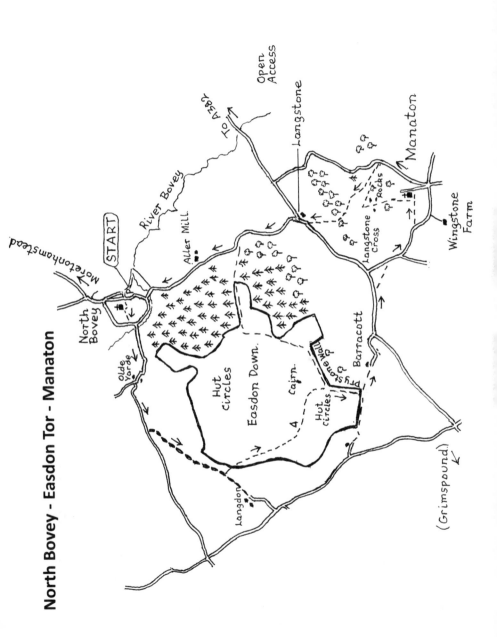

Hulbert. It has unusual statuettes above the central arch. The ancient cross standing near the west gate to the footpath has been an object of veneration. The Victorian rector objected to villagers carrying their coffins three times round the cross!

The Walk

From the Car Park enter the churchyard and head west to leave by a gate on the other side. Here a track takes you down to the North Bovey circular road.

Do not make the circle! Instead, keep on course eastwards along the lane to the right and across the River Bovey. Pass Olde Yarde and fork left. In another ¼ mile turn left. There is a sign *Byway Langdon Bridle Path to Easdon*. In 1 kilometre as the bridleway descends, turn left again to get onto Easdon Down through a gate.

Head southeastwards towards the summit where you have views over Moretonhampstead to the left and Dartmoor to the right. Then make for a cairn. Pass this on your left and continue towards a line of trees and a stone wall ahead. Go down to the dry stone wall and follow it downhill. The wall is on your left. At a T-junction turn left onto a track down to Barracot.

The little Barracot Lane takes you to the byway. Turn left and walk for ½ mile to Langstone Cross. Turn right at the sign here to Manaton, ½ mile.

If you wish to leave the lane, there is a sign on the left just before the village for a footpath across fields to the church. If you stick to the lane then you pass the track on your right to Wingstone Farm. See local Information above

From Manaton Church go to the adjacent village green with seats. Walk across to the little lane alongside. Turn left and head northeast, passing two right turns.

In just over ¼ mile turn left into a footpath on the edge of woodland. *There is a grassy driveway down on the right.* In ¼ mile ignore the track on the left up to Manaton Rocks and you come to moorland. Avoid the tempting path over the moor. Veer right to more woodland. You enter at an official marked gate and have quite a rough path where fallen branches hamper progress.

Fortunately the wood is small and you soon escape to enter a field. Climb towards a telegraph post and keep on course northwards to the lane at Langstone and white cottages.

Turn right and follow the lane back to North Bovey, a distance of 2 miles.

Manaton

4 Walks near Okehampton

Walk 23: Cheriton Bishop to Hittisleigh and Drewsteignton

A long walk north of Dartmoor with moorland type churches but softer countryside and shelter from the worst of the weather.

Starting Point: Road side parking on the lane to Cheriton Bishop Church or the nearby bus stop at Cheriton Cross.   **GR**774931   **Map:** OS Explorer 113
Terrain: Fields and lanes, moderate hills, 3 miles on 'Two Moors Way'
Distances: 10 miles the Short Walk omits Drewsteignton and has more lanes
                  12 Miles the Long Walk has three churches and more footpaths
Buses 501, 599, between Exeter and Okehampton, stop at Cheriton Cross
173 from Exeter includes Drewsteignton (Traveline 0871 200 22 33)
Local Information: Drewsteignton is high above the valley of the Teign, on the old Exeter to Okehampton Road. The village was named 'Tain Tone' in Domesday, then 'Dru' or 'Drogo', a local farmer and ancestor of Mr Drewe. The village, rich in wool, also had limestone quarries and a tin mine.
Fingle Bridge, a famous beauty spot is about 1 mile below, southeast
Castle Drogo, 1 mile southwest, was built entirely of granite, to the design of Lutyens, by Mr J.C. Drewe 1911-30. It is now held by the National Trust.
The Castle is open most of the year (not 24-26 th Dec.) Phone 01647 433306

Churches
Cheriton Bishop, St Mary is so named because a landowner, Elyanora of Melhuish gave an acre for the Bishop to build a church here in 13th century. Cheriton may mean 'Church Town'. The earlier name was 'Ceritona'. Then the Normans came and

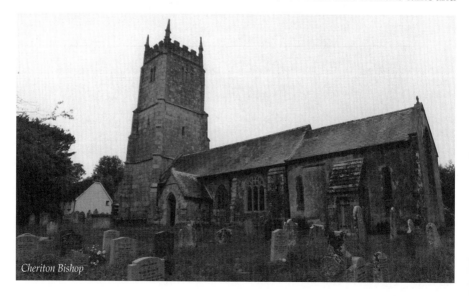

Cheriton Bishop

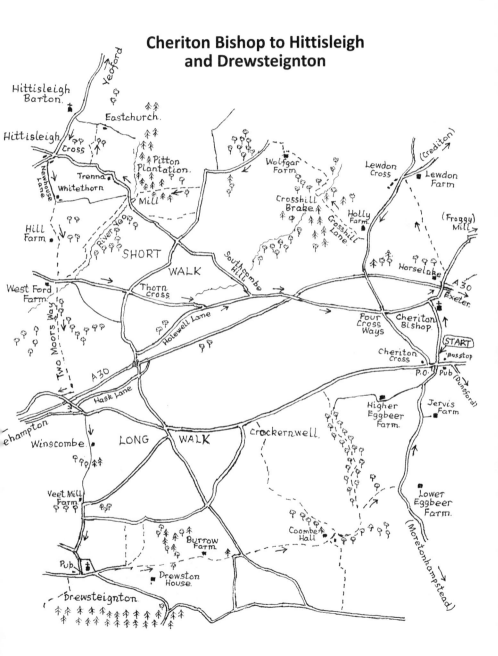

Cheriton Bishop to Hittisleigh and Drewsteignton

built a church here even before the gift of land. The sloping wall in the chancel and the font are evidence of Norman occupation. The chancel is part of the 13th century church and has lancet windows of Posbury stone. There are carved oak bosses in the ceiled chancel roof. Nave with granite piers to five bays, the north aisle and the tower are 15th century. A medieval wooden screen once extended across the width of the church. Now only the Lady Chapel is screened but there is enough to admire the beauty of the carving. The painted saints are similar to those of Manaton. The pulpit is 16th century. It has carvings of harpies and bare breasted mermaids! The coat of arms of Elizabeth 1 is above the south door, a rare treasure. Varied floor tablets are under carpet – well protected.

Hittisleigh, St Andrew, 'a farmers` church' is tucked away behind a clutch of white cottages. The peaceful granite church has a view over farmland, enjoyed by walkers along the Two Moors Way. This 'endearing little church' has Norman origins. The font with zig-zag carvings is Norman. The nave and chancel are late 13th century. The tower was added in 15th century and the north aisle in early 16th century. The walls and ceiled roofs are cream washed. There are some carved bosses. Most of the windows are simple and date from 16th century. Flagstones in the floor remember Tudor and Stuart yeomen. Two old boxed pews have been left in the north aisle. Meanwhile the 20th century has preserved this lovely church. It was re-roofed in 1967.

Drewsteignton, Holy Trinity is a dominant building facing the square. Much of the handsome old village, including one of the two pubs also gathers around the square. The original Norman church was replaced in 14th – 15th centuries by a Perpendicular building, spacious and light inside, with large windows. The south aisle and two-storey porch are embattled. This aisle may be older than the north aisle. Images of a man and a woman outside the north aisle windows may be of a member of the Courtenay or Carew families previous owners of the estate. The five arcades have plain granite piers and capitals. The windows are large and the church is spacious. The tall tower in three stages is also 15th century. The chancel was rebuilt 1861. In the churchyard is a memorial to Julius Drewe of Castle Drogo.

Drewsteignton

The Walk

At Cheriton Cross turn up Church Lane and walk for ½ mile to find steps up to St Mary`s on a slope. Continue past the church to a T-junction and turn right then left. This lane takes you to a bridge over the busy A30. Follow the sign towards 'Froggy Mill' but stop once you have crossed the main road.

Pass a turning on the left to *Horselake Farm Cottages, once a fruit farm where sadly most apples stay on the trees until they drop.* Go down to the first footpath sign on the left. Turn left into woodland and follow the path along the edge of the orchard, heading northwest. Keep on course when you leave the wood and cross six fields to Lewdon Cross.

Turn left at Lewdon Cross and follow the lane southwestwards for nearly ½ mile to the buildings of Holly Farm, a riding centre. Just after Holly Farm turn right into a farm track, Crosshill Lane. In ¼ mile the bridleway veers to the right. Head northwestwards to woodland. Climb further into deep woods that flank a stream. Go down to cross the stream and turn right on the other side. Here is another woodland path. In ¼ mile turn left to leave the woods. Head northwestwards towards Wolfgar farm, a veterinary centre.

At Wolfgar the track zigzags and you come out on the lane. Turn left and walk along the lane for 1 kilometre. After a sharp bend find a footpath on the right. This leads to Hittisleigh Mill, ½ mile away. Once again you walk through woodland and descend to a clearing. *The track to the right appears to be closed.* Take the track half left opposite, making for the River Yeo.

You soon reach the lane to Hittisleigh. Turn right and go over the little river on the road bridge. Avoid the path on the left beside the river. Instead, follow the lane climbing the steep hill past cottages on the right and then Trenna Farm on the left. In another ¼ mile, turn right into a footpath through the hedge. Continue climbing through fields following the hedge on the left then crossing through a copse to continue up through fields to Eastchurch. *The farmhouse on your right seems to be empty now and the path to the river abandoned.*

Nevertheless the driveway to Eastchurch is in fine fettle. Turn left on this driveway and walk to a T-junction with a lane at Hittisleigh Barton. *This lane leads to Yeoford to the right.* **Hittisleigh Church** is opposite.

Turn left on the lane heading down south towards Hittisleigh Cross. You have joined the long distance footpath, 'Two Moors Way'. At crossroads keep straight on. Pass a seat and the village hall on the right. Opposite a sign 'Two Moors Way', turn left into Newhouse Lane, a concrete track serving Whitehorn Farm. At the farm turn right into a field then sharp left to enter a small wood where boardwalk helps your progress.

You emerge to a winding path up through scrubland. The cottage you pass on the right is part of Hill Farm. Go through a kissing gate and you look down from a rounded hill to trees sheltering the little River Yeo at West Ford Farm. Avoid the path to the left. There are steps down to the lane.

For the Short Walk turn left here and walk up the lane for ½ mile to Thorn Cross. Keep straight on to a T-junction with Holewell Lane. Turn left. There are road signs to Cheriton Bishop. Follow these so that you head eastwards to cross the A30 on a road bridge. Keep on the road to Four Cross Ways where you turn right and walk down to Cheriton Cross. Church Lane and bus stops are on your left.

For the Long Walk (after the steps) turn right on the lane, then left to cross the rivulet and continue south on 'Two Moors Way' through woodland and up across fields. In 1 kilometre you approach the A30, turn right on Hask Lane then left for the bridge over this main road. *Hask Lane has been divided by A30, leave it behind on your left.* You are now on the road to Cheriton Bishop and have to turn right for 'Two Moors Way' to Drewsteignton. There is a prominent finger post on the right.

On the way southwards you follow the driveway to Winscombe Farm. Pass this on your left and take the footpath into a wooded valley. Go over a footbridge. The way is enclosed and goes down through trees to join a lane at Veet Mill Farm. Avoid all turnings until you come to the village square at Drewsteignton, a little over one mile from the A30.

At Drewsteignton, turn left into the Square. The pub, The Drewe Arms is on your left and the Old Inn is behind you. The Church is straight ahead. Enter the churchyard and go down steps on the right into a lane. Turn left.

In 200 metres fork left into a 'no through lane', passing houses with a good view over Drewton Wood below. The lane becomes an elevated track past a play area

before a descent to cross tracks with lovely views. Avoid a bridleway first, then a footpath, both to the left.

Keep straight on eastwards beside the edge of a field. You then descend into a wooded valley. Burrow Farm can be seen on the opposite slope. At the bottom, ford a stream on stepping stones. As you climb up towards Burrow Farm, just before a gate, you will see a small monument on the right, apparently with a lamp atop.

Drewsteignton

Pass one or two unrestored buildings on the farm then veer left on their access track. You come to a road and turn left to a T-junction.

Cross diagonally to pick up the driveway to Coombe Hall. Here are less dramatic, uninterrupted views over rolling fields. In 1 kilometre you come to the first house up a track to the left. Avoid this. Instead, go through a farm gate and down a track to a junction of paths.

Do not be tempted down the path through a farmstead on the right but keep straight on into woodland. In 100 metres at another junction, turn right and follow the leafy path on a ledge that curves to a wooded valley. Here you come to a major junction of paths. Study the signs.

Avoid the first path to the left to 'Higher Eggbeer'. Take the next path to 'Lower Eggbeer'. It climbs out of the wood and around a hillside then comes out on a lane opposite Lower Eggbeer Farm. Turn left and walk along the lane for 1 mile to Cheriton Cross.

Walk 24: Sampford Courtenay to Honeychurch

Two contrasting Churches, each with great charm are near neighbours

Starting Point: opposite Church House, Sampford Courtenay **GR**632013 **Map:** OS Explorer 113 **Terrain:** Lanes, fields and tracks, undulating **Distance:** 4 – 5 Miles
Sampford Courtenay Station at Belstone Corner has a halt at weekends on the Dartmoor Summer Service, Okehampton – Exeter. From the station to the starting point and back adds another 4 miles to the walk (See Map).
Local Information: Sampford Courtenay, a quiet picturesque village was once the scene of violent riot and murder when a mob formed to protest against the New Prayer Book in 1549. Newly built Church House should have been the centre of village festivities as wardens distributed ale. Instead disaster struck. The village lost many of its menfolk in the battles that followed and in the government reprisals.
Note: The track leading up to Beer Hill has a barrier near the top end so I have had to re-route the walk, following the lane between the two villages.

The Churches

Sampford Courtenay

Sampford Courtenay, St Andrew is a fine church, mainly early 15th century. The Courtenay family from Tiverton, Earls of Devon owned land here from 1242 and held the church. Two early possessions are the Norman font and an ancient chest, said to be hollowed from a tree trunk. The south side of the church and the tower are embattled. The majestic tower also has tall pinnacles. Inside, the nave is spacious with wide aisles and 4 large bays. Most of the south arcade is of light grey Polyphant stone. The north arcade is granite. The large windows have clear glass; some have fragments of medieval glass. The screen and east window may have been damaged in the riots. A part of the screen is in the south aisle. The ceiled wagon roofs are painted cream. There are many bosses including a Green Man, a

Sampford Courtenay - Honeychurch

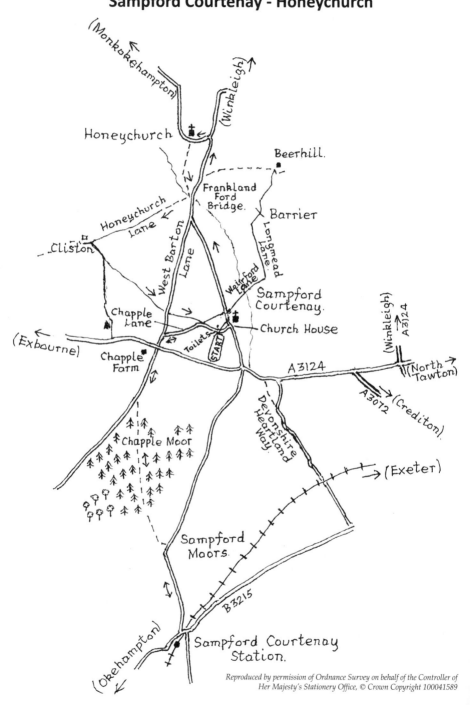

wheel of three rabbits and a sow with piglets (See also Braunton Church). This lovely church is the ideal setting for concerts and recitals.

Honeychurch, St Mary is known as the 'farmers' church'. One of them, 'Huna', possibly a 10th century landowner, gave his name to the church. The same 5 farms in Honeychurch today are mentioned in Domesday. A small Norman church, just nave and chancel, was built in 12th century. There are Norman splayed windows south in the chancel and a round-headed one north in the nave. The font is mid-12th century. In 15th century the chancel arch was rebuilt and the windows enlarged. The new roof with carved bosses and the Perpendicular tower are also 15th century. The porch was added in 16th century. After that, time stood still and no-one interfered with the plain unadulterated beauty of this gem. The medieval benches stay in place.

Sampford Courtenay

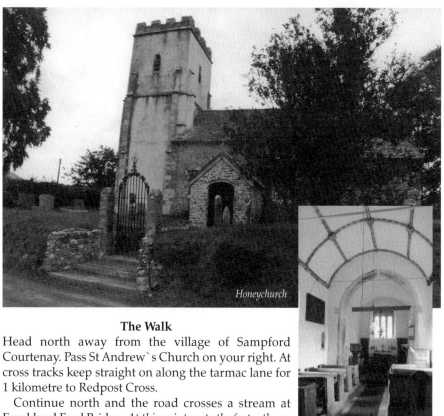

Honeychurch

The Walk

Head north away from the village of Sampford Courtenay. Pass St Andrew`s Church on your right. At cross tracks keep straight on along the tarmac lane for 1 kilometre to Redpost Cross.

Continue north and the road crosses a stream at Frankland Ford Bridge. *At this point, note the footpaths on your left for the return walk.* Meanwhile, keep on course along the lane uphill to crossroads. You have reached the hamlet of Honeychurch. Turn left for the Church.

To return from Honeychurch to Sampford Courtenay, leave the church and cross the road to the footpath opposite, part of the Devonshire Heartland Way. You are heading south to go over a hill and down towards a stream. Below, you veer left to reach the familiar road at Frankland Ford Bridge. Turn right onto the road and immediately right again into another hilly field.

Climb the hill diagonally to pass a field corner on the left. Up ahead is the western boundary of the field. There are three well spaced farmgates. Make for the middle one. It leads to an enclosed farm track leading southwest.The track is muddy in places. In 1 kilometre you reach Higher Cliston, a cluster of pretty farm buildings. **Stop!** *Avoid the footpath that leads through the farms except to take a peep at them.*

Farm, Higher Cliston

Turn left as soon as you reach Higher Cliston onto a narrow tarmac lane. *It leads to a windmill* but we leave the tarmac in 200 metres peeling off to the left and making do with a rough cart track, shaded with trees. There are occasional views over to Honeychurch on the left. In 1 kilometre at cross lanes, avoid the signed Chapple Farm to the right and go straight on for another 300 metres. You reach another set of cross lanes. *Chapple Lane is to the right. There is a dark track half left.* Avoid these and join the signed road down to Sampford Courtenay. Pass toilets on the way down. You reach the village lane opposite Church House.

Walk 25: Cookbury to Bradford

The greatest charm of this walk depends on unspoilt medieval churches

Starting Point: The village green beside the road, Cookbury   **GR**407060
 Map: OS Explorer 112   **Terrain:** Flat, muddy track and hilly roads
Distance: 4 – 5 Miles   **Advice:** lanes are usually quiet but best avoided during harvest time when tractors and trailers operate. Also avoid school run
The traffic-free track between churches is very muddy. Boots recommended.
Local Interest: The National Trust manages Dunsland, a magnficent mansion that burnt down in 1967. It is now possible to wander in the grounds among roaming cattle.

The Churches
Cookbury, St John the Baptist and the Seven Maccabees has retained its medieval character such that modern bungalows opposite seem incongruous. Forget the bungalows and steep yourself in the simple unspoilt church with tiny tower that

Cookbury

has surveyed the countryside here for at least 800 years. In 1315 a local man, Bishop Walter de Stapeldon dedicated this church. At that time some improvements were probably made. The gabled porch is 14th century. Inside, the north arcade has three bays. The eastern arch of this arcade once opened to the transept of the original cruciform church. The north aisle has an arch braced roof, possibly 16th century. The

Cookbury to Bradford

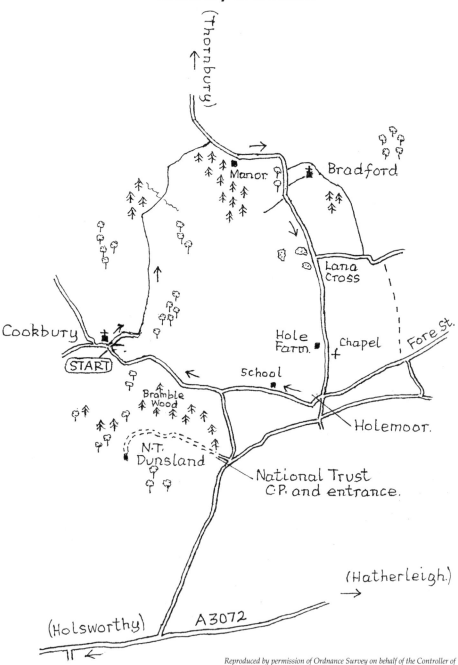

south transept with pointed arch was added early in 16th century and retains a hagioscope. There are some ancient plain benches in the nave. The 13th century chancel has late medieval floor tiles. The east window of around 1300 has three lights with trefoil head. The square font is also 13th century. In 20th century English Heritage gave a grant for the repair of the roof. In 1987 it became a Chapel of Ease to Bradford. The unusual dedication rings a shocking bell: in 168 B.C., 7 children and their mother were murdered by Antiochus, King of Syria.

Bradford, All Saints stands on a Saxon site. Later a Norman church was built and gave a 12th century circular font and south doorway with colonnettes. Most of the

Bradford

church is 14th century. The chancel window dates from around 1300. Later additions are the 15th century north arcade and Perpendicular windows in the north wall. The tower was rebuilt in 1550. Memorials to local families include Arscotts and Bickfords, former owners of Dunsland House. Tiles in the floor of the nave are 17th century from Barnstaple. The church was neglected in the early 19th century when it was home to pigs and chickens. There have been two Victorian restorations. Mary Ann Cohen from Dunsland gave the glass of the north aisle east window. There are a few old bench ends. Today all is treasured and much care is given to this attractive church.

The Walk
With Cookbury Church on your left, walk on the village lane beside the green. Pass a few individual houses. The lane bends right and becomes a wide track lined with hedges and trees and glimpses of the fields on either side.

The track is very muddy in places. It heads north for 1 kilometre then bends right, crosses a stream then becomes drier as it approaches the Bradford road.

Turn right when you reach the road, almost as
deserted as the track but with a welcome tarmac
surface. Pass Bradford Manor on the right. Ignore a
footpath on the left. You come to a white cottage on
the left. A large stone cross in front of the cottage
informs you that the Church is nearby. Walk up the
driveway to the lychgate and spacious cemetery of
Bradford Church.

From Bradford Church return along the driveway
and turn left on the road to continue on your way.
Head due south on the road for 1 mile, ignoring
turnings to right and left. Opposite Hole Farm you
pass a chapel, under repair at the time of writing. You
then have to climb up to busier roads at Holemoor.
Fore Street passes through this hamlet.

Bradford

We escape this thoroughfare by turning right into the lane back to Cookbury. In
350 metres pass the school and community centre on the right. *If you have come at
the right time you will avoid the school run.* In another 350 metres you come to a turning
on the left.
Dunsland National Trust entrance is at the end of this road, about 450 m

A better option might be to continue towards Cookbury. In 450 metres you come
to a wide entrance with a barrier to keep out cars. Here you can walk to Bramble
Wood on the edge of the estate.

Return to the Cookbury road and you have a steep climb back up to the village.

Lane betweenCookbury and Bradford

Walk 26: Abbots Bickington to Sutcombe

These churches in remote rural Devonshire have avoided over restoration but footpaths have also escaped attention and present a challenge

Starting Point: the grassy space signed to the church, Abbots Bickington **GR**383134
Map: OS Explorer 126 **Terrain:** Lanes and footpaths with some steep slopes, some bog, some rough scrub where footpath disappears
Distance: 7 Miles + 2 Miles if you decide to play safe and walk only on lanes following the Lanes Route.
Rivers: This walk is between the Rivers Torridge and Waldon, sadly unseen
Warning: The footpath between these churches can be dangerous after wet weather, especially in winter. There is a bog and pitted rough ground where footpath signs are hard to find. 'Wind blasted hedgerows' abound (Simon Jenkins). No Pub; no shop in either village.

The Churches

Abbots Bickington, is an ancient hamlet; 'Bichetone' in Domesday. It was a cell of Hartland Abbey until the Dissolution in 1539. Court Barton, next door is where the Abbot held his courts. **St James** is one of the smallest churches in Devon; nave, chancel, south transept and tower with a little spire on top, unusual in Devon. Building began around 1300 using stone rubble. It has lancet windows and original

Abbots Bickington

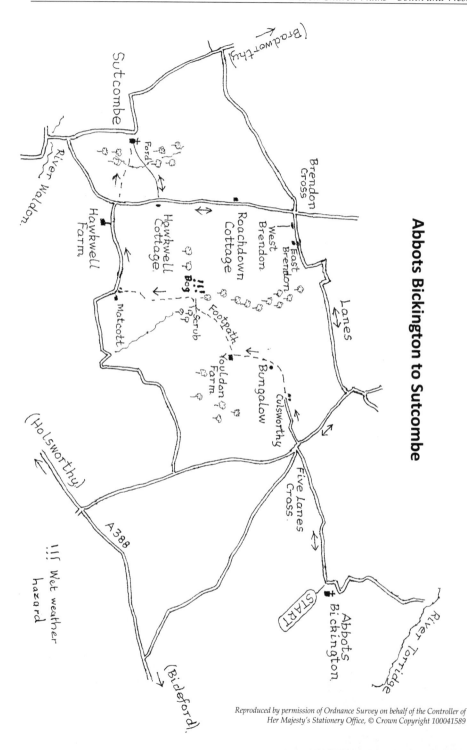

Abbots Bickington to Sutcombe

piscina. Little has changed over the years. There are old tiles from Barnstaple in the chancel floor. The medieval glass in the east window is somewhat jumbled but St Anthony and a pig are on one side and St Christopher on the other. The colourful monument to Thomas Pollard, natural son of Amyas Pollard is in a corner of the chancel. The Pollards once resided in Bishops Nympton and downsized to Court

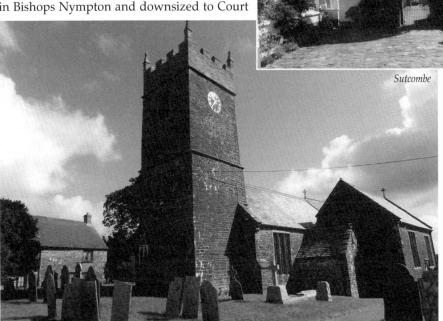

Sutcombe

Barton 17th-18th centuries. In 19th century Mark Rolle owned much of the estate and he donated a new roof and seats.

Sutcombe, St Andrew is a larger more complex church. Looking from the outside to the east end you see three large windows giving a false impression of considerable size. The simple south doorway is Norman. The rest is 15th or early 16th century. Once again medieval Barnstaple tiles are on some floors. Inside, you find the south arcade is shorter than the north. Tudor windows with square heads are in the north wall. Some medieval glass is in the east window. There are slender granite arcades and a wealth of woodwork. The remains of the well restored rood screen has some original lower panels. The pulpit has glorious carvings including sea creatures on its 16 sides. Many bench ends in the nave are 16th century in pristine condition. Mainly they depict coats of arms of local families including the Prideaux who lived at Theuborough, mentioned in Domesday.

The Walk

At Abbots Bickington stand in the grassy space with your back to the Church and turn left. Walk along the lane eastwards for 1 kilometre to Five Lanes Cross.

Footpath Route *suitable only in dry weather. See Warning above.*

**Waymarkers may have been reinstated after my request.*

Cross to the lane opposite leading to Culsworthy (no through road for cars). In ¼ mile after two houses on the right, the lane becomes a track with footpath arrows. After passing Youldon Bungalow, the track veers left.

The track ends at Youldon Farm. **There are no footpath signs* but you may find yourself greeted by large barking dogs. They did not actually attack us! If you can find anyone, he/she may admit that the footpath continues along another grassy track through the farm gate on the right.

It heads southwest for over ¼ mile and ends in a cultivated field **with no footpath sign.* Cross diagonally left down to the wooded edge of the field with a stream to cross. Keep on course (if you can) over tussocks in scrub. You may eventually find the nearby stile in the hedge (with a footpath arrow!) leading to open country. *Your problems are not over.*

Officially the path crosses diagonally left towards a hedgerow but you may have to pick your way through bog first. Perhaps less hostile if you turn left and walk round the edge of the field. Your aim is to reach the farm and manor at Matcott in view up on the hill, slightly to the left. Once you have overcome the bog, the way is easy, crossing fields diagonally left as you climb to Matcott and go through to the lane. Turn right.

Walk along the lane for ½ mile. Shortly after Hawkwell Farm, you come to a T-junction and cross diagonally right to a footpath. This path is well signed across a small field into scrub. At a grassy space encircled with trees, go to the left hand corner and follow the narrow path down to stream bed. If you find the brambles and rough terrain daunting, remind yourself that the river banks are rich in biodiversity! There is a board walk over much of the wetland followed by a long steep climb through trees to the Church at Sutcombe.

The Lanes Route. At Five Lanes Cross turn right towards Bradbury. In under ½ mile turn left towards East and West Brendon. You pass these farms after a bendy mile and reach further crossroads, Brendon Cross. Turn left towards Holsworthy. This is a busier road but has the advantage of a verge on the left and good views over the hedgerows. In 1 mile downhill turn right into a track opposite Hawkwell Cottage. I failed to find a name on this cottage but you cannot miss the kink in the road here. The track leads down to a ford which you cross using the bank on the left. Then climb up to Sutcombe a hamlet of few houses. There is a seat on the right and the Church is up on the left.

To return to Abbots Bickington (both routes), walk down the no-through-road that leads behind the church past few houses to the track to the ford.

If you came on the Lanes route, you are retracing your steps.

The way down is steep and so is the way up on the other side. Turn left on the lane past Hawkwell Cottage. Walk up this straight road for 1 mile. Turn right at crossroads. Pass West and East Brendon. In 1 mile turn right to Five Lanes Cross. Turn left for Abbots Bickington.

4 Walks Near Plymouth

Walk 27: Plymouth Churches

This is a short urban walk to Plymouth Sound visiting three churches that survived the blasts of war in different ways.

Starting Point: Plymouth Train Station   GR476553
Map: OS Explorer 108 Also free map from Plymouth City Council (Cycling) available at TIC. **Terrain:** Urban, gentle slopes   **Distance: 3+** Miles *You may choose to divert from the route to visit other iconic centres in Plymouth.*
Armada Way was formed after the Second World War flattened Plymouth. This pedestrian way sweeps down through the city, a delightful corridor of landscaped gardens and water features. It is the first pedestrian shopping avenue in England and perhaps the loveliest!
The Barbican was the harbour gateway to a vanished castle. It is now the name for Plymouth old Town where Tudor and Jacobean houses stand in cobbled streets. New Street had a medieval monastery until the Dissolution.
Stella Maris (page 119) is a marble statue taken from a wrecked ship and elevated to the walls. She was the patron saint of mariners.
The Citadel was intended by Charles 11 as a fortification guarding against enemies from the sea and the enemy within, the Plymouth Puritans who had fought against his father. It is a fine 17th century stronghold.
The Hoe or 'Hawe' means a high ridge. It is here that Francis Drake played his famous game of bowls in 1588 when the Spanish Armada was sighted.

The Churches
The Minster Church of St Andrew is a beautiful majestic building that could be a

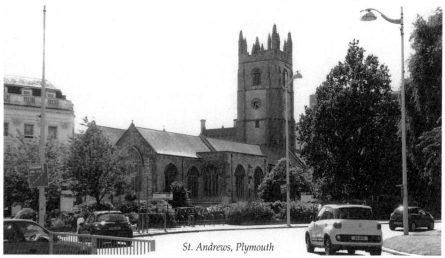

St. Andrews, Plymouth

Plymouth Churches

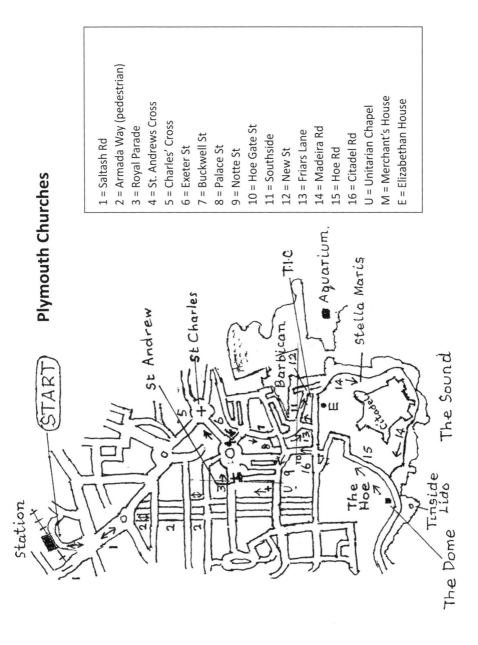

1 = Saltash Rd
2 = Armada Way (pedestrian)
3 = Royal Parade
4 = St. Andrews Cross
5 = Charles' Cross
6 = Exeter St
7 = Buckwell St
8 = Palace St
9 = Notte St
10 = Hoe Gate St
11 = Southside
12 = New St
13 = Friars Lane
14 = Madeira Rd
15 = Hoe Rd
16 = Citadel Rd
U = Unitarian Chapel
M = Merchant's House
E = Elizabethan House

cathedral. It is now the largest parish church in Devon. It was originally a little Saxon church serving the fishing village of Sutton and protected by the Hoe from pirates. St Andrew is the patron saint of fishermen. Under Norman rule, Plymouth was one of 26 parishes given to Augustinian Plympton Priory. Canons from the Priory appointed vicars and took the income. The present building dates from the 14th century when it was cruciform. The south aisle was added in 1370s and the north aisle in 1439 making it rectangular. The west tower was built in 1480s. The townsfolk paid for the stone and a wealthy merchant, Thomas Yonge had it built. St Andrews has been restored three times, in 1824, in 1875 and in 1957 after severe war damage. Outside the blitzed north door someone wrote 'RESURGAM' – 'I will rise again'. Now the church has risen again, the word appears above the north door of this reconstructed Perpendicular church. It has risen again in great splendour with the most magnificent windows; tracery renewed and filled with glass by John Piper. See the Walk Guide on sale in the shop for more details.

Charles The Martyr, Plymouth In 1641, Charles 1 reluctantly granted permission

Charles The Martyr, Plymouth

for a new church in Plymouth. The Puritans in the town wanted a break from St Andrews. Church building was incomplete when Civil War broke out. Men ran to defend the town from Royalists, abandoning the roofless building. They completed the work after the war creating a Gothic building with Perpendicular windows and Decorated east window. The 17th century pointed doorway of the south porch can still be seen. The west tower was added in 1652. The wooden spire blew off and was replaced with a stone spire in 1768. The popular preacher Dr Robert Hawker drew crowds to this church in 17th century. 8 daughter churches were built in 18th century. During the Second World War, 20th March 1941, the church was gutted. It was partially restored as a monument in 1952. Once again the church has no roof and makes a dramatic statement on the destruction of war.

Notte Street Unitarian Chapel was built in1958 after the destruction of the Treville St Chapel in 1941. The 1831 plaque, saved from the ruins of the former chapel, is on a side wall. The present building, designed by Louis de Soissons, is a neat square little chapel in neo Georgian style and has not been altered over the years. It has a slender central spire. The nearby Catherine Street Baptist Church is by the same architect.

The Walk

From Plymouth Train Station turn right at the access drive and then left onto the pavement beside the Saltash Road. Follow the crowd to two underpasses that lead to the wide, green, pedestrian Armada Way, sweeping down towards the sea.

When you see the tall tower of the Guildhall on the left, you have reached Royal Parade. Turn left here. St Andrews Church is just past the Guildhall.

From St Andrew's Church exit on the Royal Parade again and turn right. Walk to the nearby roundabout, St Andrew`s Cross. Go to the Post office in Exeter Street. Continue to Charles Church on a traffic island, Charles Cross

Return on the other side of Exeter Street to St Andrew`s Cross and turn left into Kinterbury St leading to Buckwell St. Continue down and turn right into Palace St. Pass Merchant`s House on the right. Palace St curves left to a T-junction with Notte St., a busy thoroughfare.

Turn left on Notte St. then right into Southside. You are now entering the old town, the Barbican.

At the Harbour bear right to cross New St to the Tourist Information on the right. Mayflower Steps are on the left but avoid the Marine Aquarium.

Keep walking along the seafront, passing the landing stage for boat trips on the left. You are walking along Madeira Rd, Look out for the statue, Stella Maris up on the wall on the right. You climb up beside the steep wall of the Citadel on your right.

At Hoe Rd turn left along the cliff side with a view down to Tinside Lido, now restored. Then enjoy the wider view across the Bay to Drakes Island.

Opposite the walkway down to the Lido, there are steps up on the right beside the sumptuous restaurant, the Dome. Climb these steps to Plymouth Hoe. Here you can wander forever, enjoying the bracing sea breezes and recognising the iconic landmarks of this famous stretch of coast.

From the Hoe veer right over the grass passing the entrance to the Citadel on the right. You are walking above and parallel to Hoe Road. Cross to Citadel Road then along Hoe Gate St back to Notte St.

Turn left and walk along Notte Street past the Unitarian Church. Turn right to Armada Way and head north all the way up to the Station.

Walk 28: Bere Ferrers to Maristow House

From a riverside village and fascinating church off the beaten track walk beside the River Tavy to cross a dam. A café and secret church are on the other bank. **Check tides to be sure you can cross the River,**

Starting Point: Bere Ferrers Station on the Tamar Valley Line   **GR**453636
Map: OS Explorer 108 **Terrain:** Some hills, riverside   **Distance:** 6½ Miles
Trains run every 2 hours between Plymouth and Gunnislake, stopping at Bere Ferrers. This village lies between two mighty rivers, the Tamar and the Tavy. The Train is the best way to access Bere Ferrers. .
Local Information: 1. Bere Ferrers Station is home of Tamar Belle Railway Heritage Centre where you can actually find accommodation in authentic 1930s carriages **Phone** 07813 360066
2. Lopwell Visitor Centre Café overlooks Lopwell Dam at the upper tidal mark of the River Tavy. Steep wooded banks, salt and freshwater marsh, a variety of wildlife including otter, kingfisher and salmon, all make this place special. **Phone** 01566 771930.
Check tides for river crossing (Two hours either side of High Tide)

The Churches
St Andrew's Church, Bere Ferrers stands above the river estuary of the Tavy, a strategic position to contend with invasions of Danes. There is some evidence of a Saxon church southeast of the present building. Bir or Bere means a point of land and Birlanda was the Saxon name for this peninsula. Land was awarded to Henry

Bere Ferrers

Bere Ferrers to Maristow

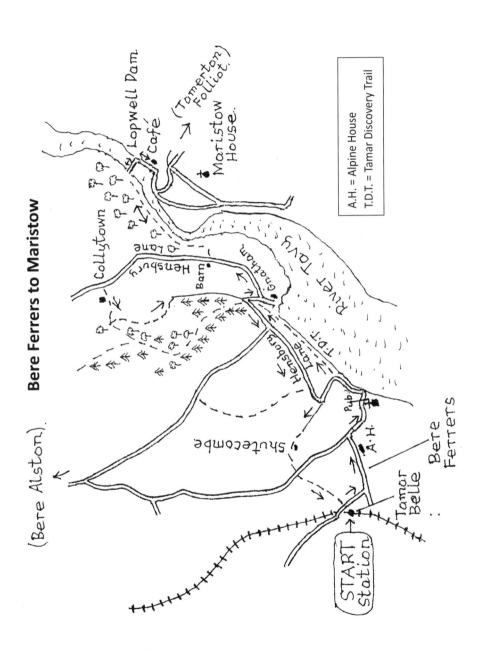

A.H. = Alpine House
T.D.T. = Tamar Discovery Trail

de Ferrier who came over with William the Conqueror. The Manor of Bere Barton was held by the Ferrier family in Henry 11`s time. Their house, much changed is still in the village. Sir William de Ferriers rebuilt St Andrew's starting in 1258. He created a collegiate church for arch priest and 4 priests. His grandson, another William extended the church. South aisle, Lady Chapel and west tower are all later additions. The south aisle has its originaal plastered cradle roof. The church should be impressive, rising as it does above the river, but the thin tower and the rough cast covering the stone detract from the beauty of the building. Inside, centuries past have created a beauty that takes your breath away. A 14th century arch divides the north transept from the nave. A knight in chain armour rests in an arch under the north window. He is thought to be Sir Reginald Ferrers circa 1300. A tomb in the centre of this transept is of Robert Willoughby 1522. The chancel is spacious. The effigies in the Easter Sepulchre are believed to those of the original founder and his wife, Isolda. The glass in the east window was given by the second William de Ferrers. There is a colourful depiction of Christ. Below three horse shoes are part of the Ferrers coat of arms. As in Exeter Cathedral, the glass was imported from Rouen at great cost. Most windows in the church have plain glass, so the eye is drawn more to the varied tracery. See the Church History and Guide for a fuller account. Other treasures include a Norman font and Tudor bench ends.

St Martin's Chapel, Maristow has a spire that beckons over the water. Only as you draw closer do you realise that the Chapel is enveloped in the buildings of Maristow House. Just east of the present building stood an ancient chapel belonging to the canons of Plympton in 14th century. It was granted to the Champernownes in 1544. In 1760 the Heywoods built a Georgian mansion here, replacing an earlier

Maristow

house. Manasseh Masseh Lope, born in Jamaica to a wealthy Portuguese Jewish family, bought the estate in 1798. The chapel here today was built in 1877 in Decorated style. It has a 5-light east window in that style. There is a three bay arcade at the west end. After a fire in 20th century the house was converted into private homes. Nevertheless, services at the Chapel are open to the public. On the third Sunday of each month you can attend at 6.30 p.m.

The exception is in December when there is a Monday Carol Service.

Phone The Maristow Estate Office 01752 695945 for more details.

Maristow

The Walk

From Bere Ferrers Station join the nearby road down towards the village. **Note** footpath sign in the **driveway** on the left. Pass bungalows. In 150 metres turn left at T-junction and continue downhill. *The way is still lined with bungalows and houses. One of these, Alpine House sells plants, honey, postcards and oddments, also hairdressing!* In 300 metres you reach another T-junction and turn right. This is Fore Street. You are now approaching the quayside village. At the war memorial veer right for **Bere Ferrers Church.** Return to the war memorial and continue down to the Quay, passing the pub, Olde Plough Inn on the way.

There are seats scattered on the grassy quayside to tempt you to sit and watch the ebb and flow of the Tavy estuary.

At Bere Ferrers Quay turn left and walk on the road beside the estuary. In 100 metres the road, Hensbury Lane veers left. You keep straight on along a track (Apple signs indicate the Tamar Discovery Trail). Your path, sheltered by shrubs and trees, passes the sports field and follows the banks of the Tavy for nearly 400 metres. *We encountered only one muddy patch in June.* The path rejoins Hensbury Lane and is accompanied by a stream on the right.

Turn right and follow Hensbury Lane to a sharp bend at Hallowell **Note** there are 2 paths on the left. Avoid these and continue on the road uphill.

The turning down to the right leads to Gnatham Farm where the owner admitted she had had to rescue ramblers who, map in hand, are misled into thinking they can continue beside the Tavy. You will flounder this way.

So, keep going uphill on the hedge-lined lane towards Collytown. In 500 metres you come to a barn on the left. Turn right into an unmarked track. It bends left and leads down towards the river on a wooded cliff. At a gap in the trees you can look across to Maristow House and Chapel, a pink vision.

In 400 metres you are at Lopwell Dam at the head of the estuary.

Salt and fresh water meet here and canoeists were enjoying the shallows.

Cross on the double line of flat stones to the other side of the river where Lopwell Visitor Centre awaits you serving teas, light lunches and icecreams.

Unless you have arrived at 6 p.m. on the third Sunday of the month, you will be unable to visit St Martin's Chapel. You can view Maristow House from a distance by turning right from the Visitor Centre then branching left uphill.

Retrace your steps over the Dam and up the unmarked track back to Hensbury Lane. **The easy route** *is to turn left and follow Hensbury Lane back to Bere Ferrers.*

The challenge is to turn right on Hensbury Lane. *This is also the cycle route of Tamar Discovery Trail.* In 1 km you come to Collytown, a large farm. Turn left into the farmyard and pass the farm on your right. Continue on a rough track to pass an adjoining footpath, go through a gate and cross a field diagonally left to another gate and take the woodland track down back to Hallowell. You arrive on one of the 2 **Noted** footpaths above.

Turn right, pass the riverside path that brought you here earlier and keep on the road for 700 metres. Avoid a road and a bridleway, both on the right.   Shortly after the bridleway, turn right towards Shutecombe. Pass the entrance to a large garden and climb the steep slope up past cottages. Only turn left when you reach a field. Follow the field boundary on the left and seek a stile in the corner. Cross to an overgrown narrow path, luckily short. Then you are on a dusty farm track. Turn left and go down to the road. *This is the road to Bere Alston.*

Cross diagonally left to a footpath. Cross a mountainous stile into a straitjacket of an electrically fenced path. It leads you up to the gate to paradise: a woodland garden. Do not Stray! Follow the **driveway** round past houses to the road. Bere Ferrers Station is to the right.

Walk 29: Brixton to Wembury

An inland walk to a seaside church with a view of the Mew Stone. Bus back, either from Wembury or along the coast from Noss Mayo or Newton Ferrers

Starting Point: Brixton Church (bus stop nearby)   **GR**554522   **Map:** OL20
Terrain: Follow Erme-Plym Trail along lanes and footpaths, over hills steep and gentle, through woodland, housing estate   **Distances:** 5, 6 or 8 Miles
Bus 94 'Tally Ho' leaves Plymouth Bus Station 8.50 and 10.50. Get off at Brixton Church. To return **Bus 48** leaves from Southland Park Road, Wembury at 2.25, 5.25 and 6.55 p.m. for Plymouth. (these buses do not go to Brixton)
Ferries: Warren Point to Noss Mayo and Newton Ferrers.
April to Sept. Phone 07817 132757
Buses from here do return to Plymouth via Brixton but please check first.
Traveline 0871 200 22 33
Local Information:
River Yealm rises in Dartmoor at Stall Moor. It ends after 12 miles in a steep sided estuary. **Warren Point** overlooks this estuary with magnificent views. It has a fringe of woodland and there are Dartmoor ponies.
Mew Stone is a prominent wedge shaped island, now owned by the National Trust. 1744 a local thief lived there for 7 years. Later SamWakeham dwelt there. He was a smuggler who married Ann in Wembury Church in 1833

The Churches
St Mary`s Parish Church, Brixton is particularly interesting for the history it recalls.

Brixton

Brixton to Wembury

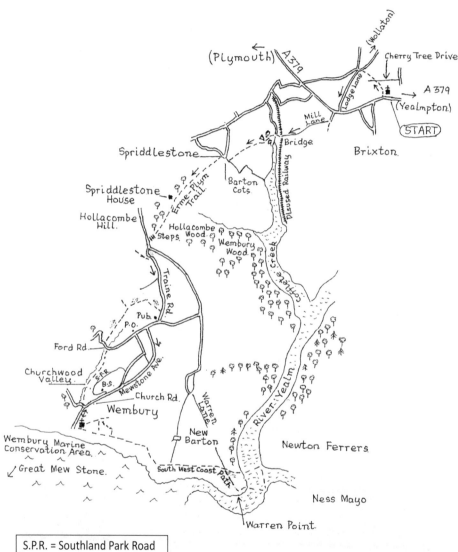

> S.P.R. = Southland Park Road
> B.S. = Bus Stop

The Saxons probably worshipped at a preaching cross here, guided by the priests from Plympton College. The Norman family of Britrickstone gave their name to the village. Plympton College became an Augustinian Priory in early 12th century with Brixton a dependent chapel. The present chancel perhaps contains the remains of this chapel. Otherwise the church is 15th century Perpendicular with an early stone tower, typical of Devon. Unfortunatly St Mary`s has lost the features retained by many Devon churches. Roof bosses, bench ends and rood screen have been destroyed. Neglect, followed by heavy Victorian restorations have taken their toll. The Fortescues of Spriddleston had a chapel in the southeast of the church and the Wood family

Brixton

from Hareston had a chapel in the northeast. Their squint or hagioscope is original. The squint in the southeast was added later. The 15th century window in the vestry came from Spriddlestone.

Wembury, St Werburgh is a good stone building with views across the sea to Mew Stone and Eddystone Lighthouse. For the Saxons this was a holy place. Today the oldest part is the 14th century square tower in two stages. The rest was rebuilt 15th –

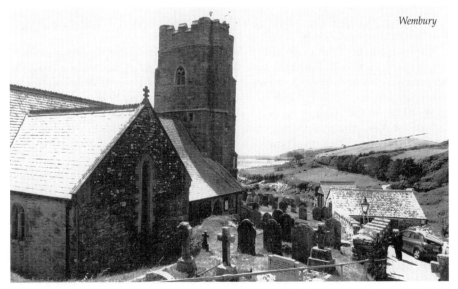

Wembury

16th centuries and consists of nave aisles and chancel. The east window of 5 lights and the west window of 3 lights are Perpendicular. The four bays of the north aisle have granite monoliths for piers. The wagon roof of the south aisle with bosses is late 15th century. The carved wagon roof over the nave is 19th century. Other good carvings of that period include south chapel screen, choir stalls, bench ends, pulpit and reredos.

The Walk

Note: There is a safe National Trust bathing beach at Wembury but car parking is impossible in the summer.

From A379, face Brixton Parish Church. The footpath on the left beside the Church is the official route of the Erme-Plym Trail leading up to Cherry Tree Drive and the road to Wollaton. Turn left here then immediately left again down Lodge Lane and back to the A379.

You can avoid this diversion by walking from Brixton Parish Church along the pavement beside A379 towards Plymouth. In 500 metres you pick up the Erme-Plym Trail. Pass Lodge Lane on your right. At a Trail sign also on your right cross the main road to turn down Mill Lane (un-named) on the left

This country lane leads to a big house – not for us! In 150 metres turn right and cross steep stiles to an elevated footpath above the sunken lane on your right. In about 350 metres the path comes down to join the lane. You pass under an unexpected railway bridge. *There was once a mineral line beside Cofflete Creek.* Avoid the gap in the hedge onto the old railway route.

Instead continue on the lane down to the head of Cofflete Creek. Turn right along the lane on the other side of the creek but branch off immediately left into a footpath climbing into woodland. In 100 metres avoid a gate ahead and scramble up the bank on the left to a stile into a field.

Keep to the right hand edge in the first field then cross the next field to steps down to a lane. Turn right.

A clutch of cottages make up the hamlet of Spriddlestone. At nearby crossroads turn left into an enclosed track with some muddy patches.

You soon emerge to the lovely arena of meadowland with tree fringes and share the pastoral view with Spriddlestone House. The stream in the centre marks the boundary between Brixton and Wembury. Cross to Hollacombe Wood on the far side and climb the slope that gets ever steeper until steps may help you struggle up to Wembury Road.

Turn left then immediately right into Traine Road. This goes steeply down to the edge of Wembury. The Erme Plym Trails takes a turn to the right but I have preferred to continue down the lane to the Odd Wheel Pub.

From the pub turn right on the main road then immediately left to Mewstone Ave. This suburban road takes a steady downward course to the sea with the Mew Stone in sight. Look out for Southland Park Road on the right. It is here that you can catch the 48 bus to Plymouth.

Avoid all turnings and you come to the green coastal space. *National Trust Café is to the right.* The track across to the left leads up to Wembury Church

Either return to Southland Park Road for the bus to Plymouth.

Or the adventurous route in summer only: turn left on the Coast Path for a 2 mile walk to Warren Point and the ferry across the River Yealm to take bus 94 to Brixton and Plymouth. Check bus times before venturing across.

Walk 30: Newton Ferrers to Noss Mayo and St Peter and the Poor Fisherman

Villages on either side of Newton Creek are linked by a causeway at low tide then a downs and seaside walk brings you to the old church on the cliffside.

Starting Point: Newton Ferrers Church   **GR**550482   **Map:** OL Explorer 20
Terrain: Hilly   **Distance:** 8 Miles (can be shortened)
Bus: 94, 'Tally-Ho' leaves at 8.50 and 10.50 from Plymouth Bus Station at the time of writing. (Last return bus 16.16 from Noss Mayo tennis courts)
Phone Traveline 0871 200 22 33 to check times of buses
Local Information: 1. At low tide you can walk across the Newton Creek to Noss Mayo, saving a diversion of nearly 1 mile via Bridge End (see map).
2. In 841 a Saxon estate was established between Rivers Dart and Plym by Aethelwulf. Later the Normans took over and gave the name 'Ferrers' to several settlements. In 1160 Ralf Ferrers was lord in Newton. Martin, the last of the Ferrers died in Newton in 1399. More recently the Yonge family held sway. From 1729 until 1940 all rectors were appointed by the Yonges.
3. Noss Mayo in the parish of Stoke has seen many changes, In 1198 Richard Revel was Lord of the Manor of Stoke, hence 'Revelstoke'. In 1287 Edward 1 gave the Manor to Mathew Fitzjohn and the name, `Mathew`s Nose' became 'Noss Mayo'. In 1877 Edward Baring from Barings Bank bought the Membland Estate and created a long coastal driveway. After the Bank Crash of 1895 the house was sold and demolished.

Churches
Newton Ferrers, Holy Cross. A church was recorded here in 1084. The Norman

Newton Ferrers

Newton Ferrers to Noss Mayo

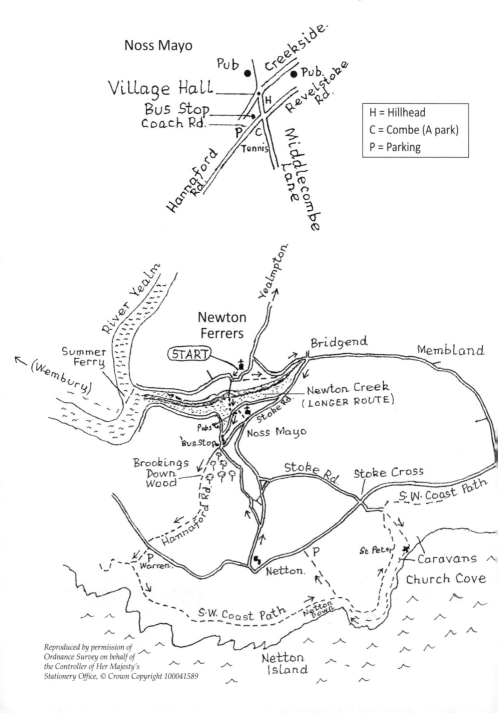

H = Hillhead
C = Combe (A park)
P = Parking

family of Ferrers held sway. They rebuilt the church early in 12th century and again in 1260. It was half the size of today`s building and was enlarged in 1342 by the rector, Henry de Ferrers. Unfortunately only the west tower, and both arcades are medieval after a thorough restoration in 1885. The tower screen has medieval bosses. There is an ancient red granite and alabaster font and a 12th century tomb lid.

St Peter`s, Noss Mayo was built between 1877 - 88 after the original village church (see below) was hit by a storm in 1868. Wealthy merchant bankers, the Barings lived

Noss Mayo

at Membland. Edward Baring, Lord Revelstoke had this church sited on a hill to stand opposite Newton Ferrers Church and yet overlooking Noss Creek. The architect was J.P. St Aubyn who has created a good solid church with local stone.

Inside, the church displays a rich Devonshire tradition of wood carving in the many bench ends and the ornate pulpit. The chancel roof has rich carvings including angels with outstretched wings. The ancient parish is 'Revelstoke'.

A Chapel of Ease in Noss Mayo was allowed for daily use around 1400 but services were still held in the old church. This chapel was absorbed into the village school. A new chapel stands at the head of Noss Creek, built in 1863. This is now the village hall.

The Church of St Peter the Poor Fisherman, Revelstoke, built in 1226 was the original place of worship for the people of Noss Mayo. Every Sunday they struggled up and down the cliffside to St Peter`s and were glad to use a

St. Peter's Noss Mayo

St Peter the Poor Fisherman

Chapel of Ease in the village. They finally abandoned the old church. Originally Saxon, it has remains from 13th – 15th centuries. The aisle and porch have carved wagon roofs. The rest is open to the sky. The Churches Conservation Trust maintains it.

The Walk

Note: *Bus 94 stops at Newton Ferrers and proceeds to Noss Mayo. At High Tide the extra mile along roads could be avoided by staying on the bus.*

From Newton Ferrers Church walk down through the churchyard to the road below. Take care, there is no pavement. Turn right.

At High Tide turn left in 50 metres at a footpath sign and pass houses on a gradual descent to Bridgend at the head of Newton Creek. Turn sharp right following the road for Noss Mayo. The Church of St Peter`s is on the right. Face the Church for a steep path on the left down to the village.

At Low Tide continue on the road below Newton Ferrers Church. Bear left opposite the Co-Op. Pass the Post Office. An open shelter faces you. Go through the door at the back to steps leading down to Newton Creek.

Cross the Creek on the flat slippery slabs to the shore at Noss Mayo and walk on

pebbles to the steps up to the pub, the Swan Inn. **For the diversion to see St. Peter's Church** turn left on Creekside Road then right. Look for the sign on the right for a steep walk up to St Peters Church. Return to Creekside Road.

If you came on the road route at High Tide, the Church is on your right and the path down is next to it.

Both routes stroll along Creekside Road and admire the quaint cottages. At the head of the Creek is a Victorian Chapel, now the Village Hall. Bear left up Coach Road towards the tennis courts on Hannaford Road. The bus stop is at the junction opposite Middlecombe Lane. There are seats in the nearby park.

Pass the tennis courts and a car park to follow Hannaford Road up through Brooking Down Wood, home to a great variety of trees. Wooden steps lead up to a steep, slippery slope emerging onto downland with views back to Noss Mayo. In 1 kilometre you come to a T-junction with the coastal lane.

Turn left to walk along the lane for 50 metres as far as Warren National Trust Car Park. Turn right into a path leading to the South West Coast Path.

In 200 metres turn sharp left to head westwards on the Coast Path. You have gentle slopes here for 2 kilometres. Pass an old lookout building, go over Netton Down *where you might see seals basking off Netton Island.* Look on left for another escape path back to the road for the return walk. Ignore it for the moment and head down to scrubland and you will find a sign on the right to St Peter's Old Church. *Ignore this also.*

The Coast Path passes through woodland above Church Cove. At crossroads turn right down a steep drive to caravan sites. Follow the drive round to the right for the **Church of St Peter the Poor Fisherman** on the cliff side.

The exciting way back is to follow the track past the Church and through another caravan site. At the end of the site, a path curves left and takes you on a grassy swathe around Stoke Point just above the sea. Eventually you have to turn up to the Coast Path above. At inlets called Three Holes, I found a narrow path through low gorse and battled my way up. Turn left on the Coast Path. As you leave the scrub for open downland, turn right to climb the slope with a fence on the right. This is your escape path (see above).

The safer way back is to retrace your steps in woodland to the escape path.

The escape path leads back to the road at another National Trust car park. Turn left and walk 450 metres along the treelined tarmac as far as buildings at Netton Farm. Turn right towards Noss Mayo then in 250 metres left into a quiet shady back lane, Middlecombe Lane on a pleasant gentle downhill slope to the bus stop in Noss Mayo. Tennis courts are on the left, the creek to the right.

See `Devon Church Walks – North and East` for Bibliography.

Some Long Distance Footpaths in Devon

South West Coast Path 90 Miles in North Devon and 115 Miles in South Devon
The whole trail following the coast around Dorset, Cornwall, Devon and Somerset, at 600 Miles, is the longest in Britain.

Tarka Trail 180 Miles long has two loops, north and south from Barnstaple. It follows the course of Tarka the Otter, based on the novel by R.Williamson

Devon Coast to Coast 117 Miles from Plymouth in the south to Ivybridge, accompanied by Erme Plym Trail then north to Lynmouth, accompanied by **?**

? Two Moors Way 100 Miles from Wembury on the south coast, through Ivybridge, across Dartmoor to Drewsteignton. It then crosses mid Devon to West Anstey linking Dartmoor with Exmoor and Lynmouth in the north.

Exe Valley Way 45 Miles follows the valley of River Exe from the estuary in the south, through Exeter (no way marks here), through Tiverton to Dulverton, 'Gateway to Exmoor' and Hawkridge, high on Exmoor.

Devonshire Heartland Way 43 Miles from Plymouth on a devious zigzag route via Crediton to Stoke Canon where it joins the Exe Valley Way above.

East Devon Way 38 Miles from Exmouth east along the coast to Uplyme.

West Devon Way 37 Miles: Hooe Lake, Plymouth north through Tavistock and the western edge of Dartmoor, including Lydford and on to Okehampton. It overlaps Two Castles Trail for six miles near Okehampton.

Tamar Discovery Trail 35 miles Plymouth to Launceston

John Musgrave Heritage Trail 35 Miles from Torbay via Cockington, to Totnes then north to Kingkerswell and back to Torbay

Two Castles Trail 24 Miles from one medieval castle in Launceston to another in Okehampton.

Erme Plym Trail 15 Miles from Plymouth to find River Erme to Ivybridge.

Templer Way 18 Miles Teignmouth to Haytor Vale, Dartmoor. It crosses the Teign, follows the river to Newton Abbot then the Stover Canal and next the Granite Tramway to Dartmoor. **Note:** Avoid High Tide on River Teign.

Teignmouth and Dawlish Way 18 mile circular from Teignmouth Pier inland to Ideford and Ashcombe, returning to the coast at Dawlish.

Dart Valley Trail 16 Miles following the River Dart to Totnes

Plymouth Cross City Link 7 Miles between West Devon Way at Marsh Mills and Tamar Valley Discovery Trail at Tamerton Foliot

Green Way 7 Miles figure of eight, Churston, the Beach at Broadsands and the River Dart where you find *Greenway National Trust House*

Notes

Notes

Notes

Notes

Notes